AMPLIFY STUDENT VOICES

AnnMarie Baines   Diana Medina   Caitlin Healy

AMPLIFY STUDENT VOICES

EQUITABLE PRACTICES TO BUILD CONFIDENCE IN THE CLASSROOM

ascd

Arlington, Virginia USA

2800 Shirlington Road, Suite 1001 • Arlington, VA 22206 USA
Phone: 800-933-2723 or 703-578-9600 • Fax: 703-575-5400
Website: www.ascd.org • Email: member@ascd.org
Author guidelines: www.ascd.org/write

Penny Reinart, *Deputy Executive Director;* Genny Ostertag, *Managing Director, Book Acquisitions & Editing;* Stephanie Bize, *Acquisitions Editor;* Mary Beth Nielsen, *Interim Director, Book Editing;* Liz Wegner, *Editor;* Thomas Lytle, *Creative Director;* Donald Ely, *Art Director;* Georgia Park, *Senior Graphic Designer;* Circle Graphics, *Typesetter;* Kelly Marshall, *Production Manager;* Shajuan Martin, *E-Publishing Specialist*

PAPERBACK ISBN: 978-1-4166-3188-0   ASCD product #122061
PDF E-BOOK ISBN: 978-1-4166-3189-7; see Books in Print for other formats.
Quantity discounts are available: email programteam@ascd.org or call 800-933-2723, ext. 5773, or 703-575-5773. For desk copies, go to www.ascd.org/deskcopy.

ASCD Member Book No. FY23-4 (Jan. 2023 PSI+). ASCD Member Books mail to Premium (P), Select (S), and Institutional Plus (I+) members on this schedule: Jan, PSI+; Feb, P; Apr, PSI+; May, P; Jul, PSI+; Aug, P; Sep, PSI+; Nov, PSI+; Dec, P. For current details on membership, see www.ascd.org/membership.

Library of Congress Cataloging-in-Publication Data

Names: Baines, AnnMarie Darrow, author. | Medina, Diana, author. | Healy, Caitlin, author.
Title: Amplify student voices : equitable practices to build confidence in the classroom / AnnMarie Baines, Diana Medina, Caitlin Healy.
Description: Arlington, VA : ASCD, [2023] | Includes bibliographical references and index.
Identifiers: LCCN 2022042763 (print) | LCCN 2022042764 (ebook) | ISBN 9781416631880 (Paperback) | ISBN 9781416631897 (pdf)
Subjects: LCSH: Minorities—Education—United States—Language arts. | Public speaking. | Storytelling in education. | Educational equalization.
Classification: LCC LC3731 .B346 2023 (print) | LCC LC3731 (ebook) | DDC 372.6—dc23/eng/20221007
LC record available at https://lccn.loc.gov/2022042763
LC ebook record available at https://lccn.loc.gov/2022042764

32 31 30 29 28 27 26 25 24 23   1 2 3 4 5 6 7 8 9 10 11 12

AMPLIFY STUDENT VOICES

Foreword

Youth voice is often shaped in ways that do not empower the young speaker. Instead of having an opportunity to express ourselves and share our thoughts, we are forced into public speaking for a grade and judged with no opportunities to grow. Decisions are made without our input, showing us how unimportant our voices are. Youth are often ignored or not encouraged to engage in public speaking due to being labeled as more or less likely to talk. Our speaking ability is taken as a product of nature, not nurture.

The practices outlined in this book amplify the perspective of marginalized speakers. It challenges the reader to think about education in a way that is new or different. Educators reading this book will have a physical resource to guide and support them on their road to amplifying student voices. Emphasizing activities based in storytelling and advocacy allows students to develop real-life skills that relate to their experiences, rather than skills only used in academia. Students, when given the skills to self-advocate, may someday stand as the foundation of a culture that empowers all people to learn by prioritizing student well-being and accessible discourse.

As members of the Junior Board at The Practice Space, a nonprofit organization that helps young people and adults in the San Francisco Bay Area develop authentic, clear, and engaging voices through public speaking, we were invited to write this Foreword and offer our own experiences related to this book. Each of the following stories comes from an individual Board member, all past participants in The Practice Space programs, about how The Practice Space has affected our lives.

This book is important to me for a few reasons. First, because I think it will help kids who are struggling to find themselves feel comfortable in school. If you spend eight hours a day within a hostile community, or a place where you feel like you can't express who you are or what you need, it has a big impact on your mental well-being. Plus, you're never going to be able to learn in a classroom where you feel stupid asking questions or that your opinion and experience aren't valued. Second, I've realized that advocating for myself and expressing my needs are some of the most important skills I've developed. The Practice Space and the authors of this book taught me to feel comfortable speaking like myself. This foreword and much of this book are the result of the collective voice of many different young people whose lives have been changed by being a part of The Practice Space programs. We hope that our classrooms will change to reflect the desire of youth to be heard.

—Amber Crenna-Armstrong, university sophomore

Everything can teach a lesson, and in this way, anywhere can be a classroom. This book is everything the traditional classroom needs more of in one place. It channels The Practice Space's values of education through speaking and about speaking in a way that emphasizes minority voices, and allows readers and teachers to incorporate this into their daily lives. Speech and debate skills are not a matter of performance or competition: they're a matter of self-advocacy, another crucial value that is key to making both students and teachers feel more comfortable in open discussions. It can be bizarre to think that a book, in printed words, can share traditions and lessons that are often orally shared. However, oral traditions can become exclusive and elitist without a reference point like this book, which ensures accessibility to all who read it. There'll always be much to learn in the world of public speaking and youth advocacy, but a lot of it can be found right here.

—Gloria Zearett, high school senior

Public speaking is one of the greatest forms of art I've ever encountered. The art of public speaking is so beautiful that I never want to lose the connection I have with it. This connection started with The Practice Space. As over-dramatic as this might sound, speech and debate changed my life. It allowed me to grow from a 7th grader whose life felt as if it was on repeat, who struggled to get through each day knowing that tomorrow held nothing new. I became an empowered, opinionated, and confident young woman. This is the power of public speaking. The ability to think in complex ways and the ability to present yourself in a whole new light is only part of what speech and debate has to offer. I believe that every student deserves to see the beauty of speech and debate for themselves. I believe that every educator should try to implement this art into their teaching so they could open their students to this whole new world. Speech and debate has taught me skills that go beyond what anyone can imagine.

—Mistura Bankole, high school sophomore

Speech and debate has been very beneficial for me: from learning the art of communication, to the art of writing and public speaking. It encourages me to be creative, think critically, and build connections. By allowing students to broaden their knowledge on a topic, practice speaking, gain confidence, and build relationships, all these benefits will be even more pronounced in the classroom. I can go on and on about all of the benefits of speech and debate in my life, but let me just say this: the skills learned will be applicable anywhere in life.

—Mercy Niyi-Awolesi, high school sophomore

The Practice Space helped me find my passion—learning about communication. The Practice Space also aided me in finding my voice and taught me how to use it. Now that I have graduated, I am working as an Administrative Assistant in a college housing office and am able to use all that I have learned. I feel more confident sharing my opinions and thoughts with my superiors on projects and I am able to articulate myself to students and parents. I believe I would never have found myself on this path had it not been for The Practice Space. It helped me grow as a professional by giving me the opportunities to work on communicating, speaking without judgment, and learning from my mistakes.

—Lindsey Lam, college graduate

My first dedicated speaking experience came from The Practice Space. While I had been exposed to speaking, largely through school projects, it was the first time I had been introduced to a space where speaking was the focus. When I remember those first experiences, I remember a feeling of warmth. I was encouraged to do what I wanted and made to feel successful for trying out new things. I was surrounded by a community of people who taught me how speaking could be fun! Because I was encouraged to speak at The Practice Space, I began to feel more capable and more confident in myself. I was certain that no matter what I did there would be this lovely community there to support me. It made me value my own originality in speaking, not simply parroting the group view but bringing a unique perspective.

—Will Flowers, high school senior

The Practice Space empowered us to make our own choices in how we communicate. It taught us skills that we can use in the classroom in middle school, high school, and college—even into our professional careers—to advocate for ourselves and express our opinions to others. Our experiences with The Practice Space have made us more confident, competent speakers.

This book outlines how to uplift marginalized voices in the classroom within a framework that interweaves storytelling, poetry, and informative speech. It provides tools for educators to use to introduce all their students to public speaking and help them feel comfortable. It exemplifies how teachers can use their experiences to connect with their students and a learning environment based on valuing individual identities and experiences, while encouraging students to be ambitious and passionate.

The practices and teachings discussed in *Amplify Student Voices* have shaped us into experienced communicators and can help educators guide their students into becoming skilled, expressive speakers.

—Mistura Bankole, Mariana Castro,
Amber Crenna-Armstrong, Will Flowers,
Lindsey Lam, Elohiym Mudaavanha,
Mercy Niyi-Awolesi, Michael Schoonover,
Gloria Zearett

Introduction

Vergüenza (shame)

A Latino parent's favorite social construct
The finger that always pointed to tradition
The internal voice that told me what was expected
The reason my parents reprimanded me
when I stirred the pot, when I asked for things,
when I took too many liberties in being myself
This set of beliefs kept me in line
but being silent never sat right in my body
Waiting for permission to exist wasn't my style

I was taught *vergüenza* was needed
to know our place on society's totem pole
Me taking up space constituted misbehavior
Repeated reprimands felt like silencing mantras:
Eso no se hace (that is not done)
No tengas tanta confianza (don't be so confident)
Somos gente humilde (we are humble people)
Hay que tener vergüenza (you have to have shame)

I didn't understand why I needed shame
Why couldn't I be proud of who I was?
Why couldn't I ask for water when I was thirsty?
Why couldn't I be curious?

1

Why did I have to be quiet?
Why was my virtue connected to how much shame
my tiny shoulders could carry?
Hadn't my ancestors carried enough for us all?

—Diana Medina

Safety in Silence

When I was in preschool, teachers worried that I was antisocial because I would sit alone on the swings, away from the other kids. What they didn't notice was that everyone else was on the jungle gym, climbing and jumping across wooden logs, while I watched and winced when they slipped and fell. I didn't want to fall. As I entered elementary school, I kept watching as my peers took risks, keeping a mental record of what worked and what didn't. I saw how happy my teachers were when people raised their hands and gave right answers, so I studied hard so that I could do the same. I saw how speaking out of turn sent you to detention and speaking too loudly got you weird looks, so I learned to sit quietly and smile, keeping my distance from the "troublemakers."

I watched as my peers were sorted into "good students" and "bad students," and Black boys were sent to detention more often than everyone else. When I was growing up in the San Francisco Bay Area in the 1980s, the narrative of colorblindness was alive and well, and I regularly heard how important diversity and multiculturalism was, but that I also "shouldn't see color." As a Filipino American, I regularly checked the box for "Other" on forms. I learned not to see anything strange in statements such as "You're lucky because no one can tell what you are" or "I don't think of you as Filipino," and even take comments such as "Filipinos are the best because they are always smiling" as compliments. It was OK to be erased and good to be invisible, as long as you smiled and got the answers right. As an immigrant to the United States, my mother stayed quiet, fearing that if she spoke up, she would get sent back to the Philippines. Yet she also taught me you needed to earn your voice, that good grades and leadership positions meant that I could speak up.

I wanted to speak, but I didn't know how. Saying the right answers was one thing, but as time went on, I watched with envy as my peers stated their opinions in class and confidently told stories and jokes during lunch. I wanted to be like them, seemingly free from awkwardness and uncertainty. Speaking up had become much more complicated: you had to speak up, but in the right way. I needed to speak for myself, while also not saying anything wrong, upsetting, or offensive. I needed to be a leader, but I also needed to blend in. I needed to be a smiling Filipino girl, while not letting anyone think of me as different. As I figured out the rules, silence felt safer, and being quiet was the best kind of protection from falling.

—AnnMarie Baines

Silence as Oppression

For historically marginalized groups in the United States, silence is a source of oppression. Feeling free to speak remains a privilege reserved for those whose voices have been encouraged, cultivated, and valued as significant and influential. As we begin this book, our opening poem and story serve as examples of how diverse forms of expression communicate complex personal experiences that are too often pushed aside when having to adhere to accepted molds. Instead, we as authors believe in honoring the diversity of expressive styles required to reflect diverse histories and experiences, which we ourselves exemplify:

- As a Filipino American learning scientist, special educator, longtime coach, debater, and vocal performer, AnnMarie Baines combines stories and research to contextualize the experiences of those who feel invisible, misunderstood, and labeled.
- As a storyteller, educator, and poet, Diana Medina uses poetry and creative expression to communicate her identity as a first-generation Mexican American, daughter, aunt, lover of pop culture, and in-system activist dedicated to creating brave "learning containers" where people articulate their authenticity and discover the power within them.
- As an abolitionist, outdoor dreamer, and white Jewish mother, Caitlin Healy uses her background in alternative education to advocate for youth pushed to the margins by public school systems.

Together as women and products of public schools, we are devoted to creating a world where diverse communities of youth and adults feel capable, cared for, and free to use their voice in powerful and meaningful ways.

Silencing in History and Today

For centuries, having a voice has never been the default for everyone, and white supremacist and colonialist policies throughout history have driven institutionalized oppression that taught us to believe that only a few are entitled to their voice.

Many historical examples of oppression are still happening today (David & Derthick, 2018). Women and Black people in the United States were denied the vote, and voter suppression continues in modern-day elections. Indigenous children were stolen and sent to white boarding schools such as the Carlisle Indian Industrial School in Pennsylvania from 1879 to 1918 to pacify resisters who did not want to give up their land, and tribal sovereignty issues still persist. Forced family separation has continued as a strategy for domination, and U.S. history has seen the children of enslaved Black families sold at will, welfare workers taking children away from families in poverty, mass deportation of Mexican immigrants blamed for the Great Depression, people of Japanese ancestry ordered into prison camps during World War II, and the family separation policies initiated by the Trump administration at the U.S.-Mexico border, to name a few.

The long list of examples continues with the institutionalization of people with disabilities at institutions such as the Willowbrook State School in New York that became a method for isolating and imprisoning people who were not seen as worthy or human, and people with disabilities remain marginalized. Women have long battled the patriarchy to gain agency over their own bodies and decisions, as well as equal pay and opportunities. Black people have endured a history of lynching, as in 1953, when Della McDuffie was murdered by Sherriff Jenkins of Alberta, Alabama, and after demanding an investigation, her husband was found dead, causing the family to flee for their lives (CRRJ Archive, n.d.). Today, we continue to see Black lives taken by police with impunity, with George Floyd's murder in 2020 galvanizing the globe around his final words, "I can't breathe." These policies and practices are intended to silence people, and yet, in the face of such violence, people have always found creative and complex ways to resist, including using silence as one of many tactics for survival and self-preservation.

Beyond systematized policies, silencing has been taught through everyday encounters at multiple levels referred to as interpersonal, institutional, and internalized oppression, raising people to expect discrimination and even endorse it (David & Derthick, 2018). In a Duke University collection of more than 1,000 interviews with Black Southerners who lived through the Jim Crow era, an Arkansas woman, Cleester Mitchell, tells how she was treated in stores:

> If we went to a grocery store and a certain lady come in the store, a white lady come in the store or anybody white, if they was waiting on you, they'd just push your stuff back and said, come on, Miss So-and-So, and you might be walk 10 miles to get this dime worth of something that your parents sent you at, but that was like the law of the day. You know, you understand, it wasn't anything you could do about it, but it did not bother us like it would today. It wouldn't have the same effect on us because we was raised to expect this and everything. They taught you this. (Cox, 2011)

In addition to outright discrimination, everyday actions continue the erasure of cultural identities, silencing entire histories. Despite being the second-largest Asian ethnic group in the United States, Filipino Americans continue to be the product of American colonial dominance, and their stories remain untold and invisible from mainstream media and U.S. history books. The desire to fit in twists reality so people who are marginalized participate in their own silencing and can become complicit in the silencing of others (a situation known as "lateral oppression"). In his essay "How a 'Secret Asian Man' Embraced Anti-Racism,"

Filipino American Eric J. Daza (2020) documents his own reckoning with white supremacy and the effects of colonization. As he describes it, "white supremacy is not limited to white people. In my experience, it is also very Filipino." As a result of colonization, he continues,

> the Philippines became a beautiful tropical island paradise where parents warn their kids that they'll get too dark in the sun, . . . stereotypes about Black Americans persist, and skin-lightening products abound. The historical trauma known as colonial mentality—a kind of culture-wide Stockholm Syndrome towards our white colonizers—still warps *kababayan* (citizen) hearts and minds.

Schools That Oppress Instead of Protect

Schools are designed to reinforce expectations of conformity, where young people who do not fit dominant expectations are policed, labeled "at risk," pushed to the margins, ranked as less competent, and seen as less successful (Baines, 2014). These expectations, defined by white-supremacy culture, have characteristics such as the worship of the written word and the assertion that there is only one right way to do something or say something (Okun, 2021). Speaking and listening are finally included in academic standards as a means for demonstrating knowledge, but without a focus on developing self-advocacy skills that help learners express authentic identities, connect to their cultural backgrounds, and feel safe. Even when adults adjust their mindsets to become more inclusive and ability-oriented, youth can continue to reinforce damaging assumptions about their peer's capabilities. As Stanford University's Ray McDermott and colleagues highlight in their 2006 research article "The Cultural Work of Learning Disabilities,"

> Even if the teacher manages to treat every child as potentially capable, the children can hammer each other into negative status positions; and even if both teacher and children can resist dropping everyone into predefined categories, the children's parents can take over, demanding more and more boxes which specify the kinds of kids who can do better than others. (McDermott et al., 2006, p. 15)

The overwhelming sources of oppression create a reality in which keeping silent is necessary for self-preservation. In his memoir, *Children of the Land*, the poet Marcelo Hernandez Castillo (2020) recounts his experience with shame, silence, invisibility, and fear of authority as a result of being an immigrant. We also see the legacy of Chinese exclusion in the United States manifesting today in the classroom and in daily public life, as youth and adults hunker down and try not to be noticed amid anti-Asian sentiments and threats of violence.

It is hard to speak up when you have been oppressed, and it is dangerous to be vulnerable when you have always had to work even harder to keep yourself both psychologically and physically safe. The fear of public speaking, although often viewed as an individual issue, must be acknowledged in conversations about oppression. According to psychologists David and Derthick (2018), "It can be very scary to speak up or do something to resist oppression, especially since oppression is rooted in the very dynamics of power and privilege that silences voices of oppression" (p. 167).

Our history of silencing is hard to read and swallow, let alone live. When silencing has not been part of a person's life, it is easy to feel protective or to deflect responsibility to preserve one's fragility. It is tempting to avoid these hard conversations or say it isn't our job or we don't have time. But instead of silence, young people need support to find the language to speak about what they are going through, the experience they are living, the people they are becoming. They need language that retains and evolves their identities to become individuals who don't have to sacrifice themselves to be accepted. They also need environments where they can speak in a style that fits their identities and about issues they care about, without having to give up who they are to fit a dominant mold. As Toni Morrison stated in a 1993 interview,

> I'm not gonna give up one drop of melanin to get it [upward mobility]. I'm not going to erase my race or my gender to get there. I want all of it. I deserve all of it, and we all do. I don't want to be blanded, bleached out, in order to participate in this country and walk any hall of power or corridor that I want to. (Rose, 1993)

This book will tackle discomfort directly through the lived experiences of youth. It will guide both you and young people through the topic of self-expression, even when it is uncomfortable.

The brown girl in the white room

Brown girl was nervous
It was her first time in a room this white
She wondered how they let her in
She didn't know what they knew
She wondered why she was here
She felt like a fly swimming in a jug of cream

Brown girl had a special light switch
That turned on light bulbs in people's minds
with thoughtful questions at the right time
She didn't know this was a gift until someone thanked her for it
She spent her entire life looking for a place in white rooms
Trying to silence inner struggles to hear herself,
Trying to hear the room and be part of conversations
Asking questions was a way to buy some time
to silence her doubts before needing to respond

If the white room could hear her
she would finally confess:
My brain is a crowded conference room
My emotions and past selves have heated debates
They question every thought before I say it
They argue about what is wrong today
They call me an imposter
Their discourse overpowers everything
the sound of my breath moving through my nostrils
the sound of my paycheck in my bank account,
the sound of you talking about important things

My brain feels like a Zoom call from hell
I am a struggling facilitator
I am an inadequate holder of space

I try to steer these emotions towards harmony
But I fail every time so I struggle to pay attention

Maybe there is something I can do to be like you
or maybe this is what I have to deal with
because I am just a brown girl in a very white room

—Diana Medina

Excited to Speak

In the summer before 9th grade, one of my friends, Audrey, urged me to sign up for a summer debate camp with her to keep her company. Audrey was one of the cool, outgoing girls I deeply admired, who spoke up with such confidence and ease. It didn't hurt that she was mixed-race like me. I had no idea what to expect, but at least I had my friend.

On that first day, I sat back in awe as I watched experienced high school speakers demonstrate the 17 different speech and debate "events" that I could choose from, including everything from arguing about policy issues to acting out plays. When I heard about the option to write my own play or poetry, I knew I had found my place; it was the first time in my life that I had ever felt excited to speak.

From that moment on, I was hooked. Even after my friend pursued dance at another high school, I spent every weekend performing my original plays at speech tournaments. My coach vigorously encouraged me to join the Lincoln-Douglas Debate part of our high school team, a style of one-on-one debate that involved the discussion of philosophical and ethical issues. Debate was hard and terrifyingly spontaneous, and I watched and listened to my teammates rattle off opinions about Immanuel Kant and social contracts, with no idea what I should say. All I knew was that I wanted to be like them. At tournaments, I lost round after round, but each time I would go home and redo all of my rebuttal speeches in the tiny bedroom I shared with my sister in our 750-square-foot house. Debate literally filled our home.

The turning point came two years later, when my coach helped me secure a scholarship to a prestigious debate camp in Iowa. After those two weeks, I felt like I could go beyond the rules of debate and instead create strategies for my arguments, find connections to the audience, and create my own persuasive delivery style rather than imitate others'. I finally knew how to speak for myself, combining my smile with steel.

It felt good to go undefeated at tournaments at the state and national levels. It felt even better to feel like I didn't have to hang back and watch anymore. I could be strong. During my senior year, I competed at a nationwide tournament at UC Berkeley, one round away from making it to the Tournament of Champions, a goal I had been working toward all year. As the judging panel announced the results, the first gave the win to me, whereas the second voted for my opponent. The last judge sat back in his chair and said, "I voted for the guy. Because." Later, when we received the written comments, I looked at the single sentence he wrote on the ballot: "You're too aggressive for a girl."

—AnnMarie Baines

Public Speaking and Internalized Oppression

It is important to question what makes "good public speaking," as such definitions are part of deeply ingrained, Western social norms. It is challenging to distinguish the line between what is considered guidance and what is actually oppression embedded in dominant social beliefs. As UCLA professor Samy Alim lays out:

> Our sort of national language ideology is that there is a standard English, there is a proper way to speak and an improper way to speak. What we never confront is that the so-called standard English . . . is a myth. It's a construct. It's not real. It's a variety and a style of speaking that's modeled after wealthy, white, middle class, upper class, usually male, straight, heterosexual, etc. It's modeled after the dominant. It's modeled after these mostly dominant men who imagine themselves to be accentless, or to be speaking some kind of standard. You never really encounter a philosophy or thinking that challenges standard English, at least from the schooling perspective. (Gordon, 2019)

Tips and advice around the "effective characteristics or traits of public speaking" most commonly involve speaking slowly, being confident, never saying "um," and speaking loudly, along with "being yourself" and "connecting with your audience." But who is privileged by this defi-nition? Famous examples of public speaking continue to be overwhelm-ingly male, in contexts such as battlefields, boardrooms, and political stages that have been historically fraught with oppression and reserved for people who are white and wealthy. Speaking slowly and loudly alienates cultures built upon rapid storytelling or quiet, intimate con-versations. It can be hard to feel confident when you have experienced oppression and discrimination, and never saying "um" means you need to hide your uncertainty, even when English is your second language. Language is the expression of our ever-evolving identities, but it is hard to "be yourself" and "connect to your audience" when social norms and covert biases do not reflect who you are.

As David and Derthick (2018) advocate, "If there is only one thing we need to always remember about oppression, we believe it should be the fact that it is an environmental construct that is external to people" (p. 156). The fear of public speaking is too often treated as an individual problem, when public speakers are literally judged by previously held beliefs and implicit biases about how they should look or sound. "Public speaking" is still perceived as something that only happens on a stage in front of a microphone, often in front of strangers (rather than an inter-personal activity that happens constantly in everyday life in relationship to others), which also means that it takes place in the most high-risk situation for people who have been marginalized and oppressed. It makes intuitive sense that fear would differ based on personal experiences, and yet there is little to no research differentiating who is more afraid of public speaking and what should be done to combat this example of what is known as "subtle oppression," a form of oppression that is less notice-able and more easily justified or denied than others.

In her 2005 article, "Silence Speaks," community activist Vivian Chávez asks better questions: "How can people who are different from one another hear and be heard by each other? What actions must community-based researchers take at the personal and institutional levels to be better prepared to listen and respond to the silent language of internalized oppression and privilege?" (p. 9). Instead of the typical focus on fixing style and delivery, it is critically important to help people develop and establish their message, process their fears, reflect on the impact of oppression, and use their voice to challenge it. The hyperfocus on eliminating filler words denies their critical importance in the human language, which is to act as a buffer in conversation, assist thought and reaction, and communicate the real-life experiences with uncertainty that are part of authentic storytelling, so much so that many linguists argue "um" should be considered a word (Enfield, 2017). Surface-level comments about pace and volume encourage listening to criticize and draw attention away from deep, meaningful listening to the message itself. Being vulnerable in the face of oppression is scary and requires hard work, a process that should be appreciated, cultivated, and never undermined by adherence to stereotypes.

My Secret Lies

My secret lies in the lies I tell myself
Lies like: I am not good enough,
I'm just ordinary; nothing special.
No one wants or needs my opinion.
Who am I to speak and take up space?

My secrets have lied to me.
They kept me away
from my most authentic Self.
They made me blind
to my own truth and afraid
of becoming powerful.
They made me hide my spark
under eurocentric expectations.
I sacrificed my substance
in hopes of being accepted.

My secret is I am trying.
In fact, me saying 1000 ums

is the sound of me trying.
Those ums are drums playing
the cadence of my convictions
as I learn to set them all free.
The moment I learned this I settled into this skin
and it finally felt like safety.

My secret is most of the time
I don't know what I am doing.
I haven't known for decades I am so good at it.
People even listen to me.
They offer me seats at their tables.
They make space for my opinions.
They accuse me of inspiring them.

My secret is I no longer believe
in faking it til I make it.
My only focus is making it,
being it, saying it, naming it
so that I never ever have
to fake anything again.

—Diana Medina

Staying Strong

"You're too aggressive for a girl" is a statement I have heard many times since that ballot at UC Berkeley. Luckily, those statements, along with the countless racist microaggressions I also encountered, have always been drowned out by caring mentors and peers. After I looked at that ballot, my coach pulled me aside and, in the midst of my tears, said simply, "You're strong. People like that are just going to have to deal with it. You keep doing what you do." My teammates rallied behind me, expressing their outrage and sharing their own stories. The same avalanche of support came when a Black teammate was told by judges to "dress more professionally" and "speak with more polish." Beyond the tournaments themselves, education happened outside the rounds, when we had to speak up whenever we witnessed people cross the street when they saw our Black team-mates or when an Asian teammate was asked in the airport in a mocking tone, "Do you speak English?" Diversity and advocacy were part of our team identity, both in and out of rounds.

Although I was certainly taught and trained to align with many of the same dominant norms I critique, I was fortunate to have had educa-tors who always focused more on who I was and what I wanted to say. The debate camp in Iowa that made such a difference always empha-sized saying what I believed rather than what I thought the audience wanted to hear. Argument strategy was always about helping teach and explain complex issues to promote common understanding as opposed to saying something to dominate others. Although I have had coaches who squirted me with water guns until I stopped saying "um," I have also had coaches who told me that my voice was unique and that I should "speak like AnnMarie" instead of trying to imitate someone else.

I will never forget how hard it was to develop my voice. Figur-ing out what to say and how to say it with or without preparation was already challenging, especially for someone who found safety in silence. Being able to speak under conditions where people are expecting less from you requires the kind of self-belief and confi-dence that come from having a support system that teaches you that your voice is important and powerful.

More than 20 years later, I started The Practice Space in the same neighborhood I grew up in and serve the same schools I attended, so that our nonprofit could use public speaking as a way to elevate under-represented voices instead of as a way to oppress them. I continue to coach because self-expression is critically important, but it takes time, rigorous practice, and community. Young people should not be aban-doned in this process, especially in a prejudiced and racist world.

—AnnMarie Baines

Collective Empowerment to Speak

This book is for educators who care about young people—educators who, like us at The Practice Space, believe in the following statement: "Our voice is powerful because it belongs to us. Our voice is imbued with the richness of our experiences, and it is the most powerful tool we have to challenge the oppression in our world" (David & Derthick, 2018, p. 167). As the authors point out, speaking up in the face of oppression requires people to (1) rehearse, (2) anticipate and navigate defensiveness from others, (3) tell their story, and (4) enlist support.

Young people need the support of educators to create the conditions for rehearsal and practice, where they can process negative reactions, believe that their stories are powerful and worth telling, and learn to navigate and approach challenging situations and share common experiences. At the time of this writing, we are beginning to emerge from the effects of a global pandemic in a world that continues to be fraught with racial injustice and hate. It is a world that needs healing and repair within and across communities, and public speaking has an important role to play.

What the pandemic has also revealed is the enduring reality that different learners need different structures, vehicles, and forms of public expression. Many young people who succeeded in participating and engaging in person have retreated into their shells online. Many shy learners have thrived through the use of chat features, small breakout rooms, and speaking with their web cameras turned off. Countless others have embraced a world of informal, spontaneous speaking through social media and Instagram Live, while others scramble to figure out the rules of engagement in a world where the rules have all changed. As the world changes, so should communication. What remains true is that the norms need to be continuously questioned by asking ourselves who they privilege, who they silence, and why.

What to Expect from This Book

Throughout this book, we define *educational equity* as an environment that (1) reduces the predictability of success and failure, (2) disrupts inequitable power dynamics and promotes shared power, (3) maximizes opportunity to showcase strengths and interests, and (4) minimizes the impact of oppression. Equity is deepened through small moments, as an environment where stories and opinions are not a waste of time and are treated as essential to understanding experiences. Equitable teaching practices disrupt the tendency to treat people as "less than" or "other" and instead facilitate access through multiple entry points and promote understanding, a sense of humanity, and a space for learners to genuinely surprise one another. We introduce Expression-Driven Teaching[SM] as a facilitation method for creating brave classroom spaces for speaking, listening, and shifting mindsets around which voices are valued and why.

This book is for educators who teach students of all ages, and our goal is to promote the authentic expression of youth identities to combat long histories of marginalization and to avoid reinforcing inequity and oppression. The underlying principle is that advancing educational equity and challenging systemic, interpersonal, and internalized oppression require the presence of diverse voices, which can only be cultivated when diverse forms of self-expression are valued and taught. We intend for the chapters to be read in order, to first ground you in overarching methods for creating safe and brave spaces to speak and in understanding how youth experience public speaking emotionally, before going into specific techniques for how to facilitate youth voice through storytelling, debate, poetry, presentation, and self-advocacy.

In the Foreword and Chapter 1, we lean on the contributions of high school and college-age youth from our Junior Board of Directors at The Practice Space as authors who articulate the factors that silence young people, especially at school and at home. Their advice is woven throughout to communicate the reality that young people want to see in the classroom. We limit use of the term *students* to showcase them as people with identities that go beyond the classroom. The young people featured in all the chapters are teens from The Practice Space, a nonprofit founded by AnnMarie Baines to elevate underrepresented voices by building confidence and community through development of communication skills and education in public speaking. Each of them has gone through multiple years of instruction and practice to express themselves through stories, debate, poems, and speeches. The vast majority come from large, comprehensive public schools in the Bay Area, with varying academic records, an eclectic set of interests and passions, and a range of comfort levels with public speaking. Their stories are unedited and collected through interviews and written contributions. We also conducted "member checks," in which young people were able to read and give feedback on how they were represented in this book.

The remaining chapters of this book are a guide for developing confident, diverse speakers who can communicate their identities and beliefs through a range of public speaking approaches. In Chapters 2 and 3, we define the elements and facilitation strategies in the Expression-Driven Teaching framework and describe how to create the classroom conditions required for young people to feel brave and confident enough to speak. Chapter 2 also continues situating our methods in movements for educational equity and *abolitionist teaching* through discussions about threats to youth identity and expression. The concept of *intersectionality* is an important backdrop to these discussions, drawing upon Kimberlé Crenshaw's (1989) framework for understanding how aspects of a person's social and political identities combine to create different modes of discrimination and privilege.

Chapters 4 through 8 go in depth in exploring different modalities for youth expression and providing practical guidance for how to integrate them into your classroom. In Chapter 4, we discuss how to use storytelling as a method for increasing diverse representation and engaging English language learners. Chapter 5 lays out debate-centered instruction as a tool to promote equitable participation, including debate protocols, tips for structuring debates, easy warm-ups and drills, and considerations for encouraging girls' involvement. Chapter 6 shows how poetry can be used to bring emotions to life and creatively showcase individuality. In Chapter 7, we examine how to make class presentations more dynamic and authentic, including example rubrics, tips for guiding content and coaching delivery, advice on how to support listeners in giving feedback, and considerations for English language learners. We end with an in-depth youth story in Chapter 8 about the journey to develop self-advocacy skills and guidance on how to create an environment that encourages youth to speak up for their needs and experiences.

Chapters 4 through 7 include the following information:

- Equity considerations and practices related to each public speaking approach
- Guidance on how to plan effectively and how to prepare speakers and listeners
- Suggestions for coming up with equitable prompts and topics
- Practical protocols and suggested activities
- Advice or stories from youth
- Links to online curriculum resources

Efforts to dismantle systems of oppression can be discouraging and overwhelming, especially in the midst of competing demands on educators who are already exhausted by institutions that fail to support them. As community psychologist Jennifer Rudkin (2003, cited in David & Derthick, 2018) reminds us through the paradoxes of creating social change,

> The situation is urgent, so we must take our time. . . . The problems are huge, so we must think small. . . . Social change is complex, so we should keep it simple. . . . Social change is serious business, so we must have fun. We must find a community, or create a community, in order to connect with others. There is no social justice without relationships. (p. 170)

When young people have fun, communal spaces that allow them to become collectively empowered to speak, they get to do the hard work required to feel ready to speak up and lead when the moment calls for it. Before the February 2018 mass shooting at Marjory Stoneman Douglas High School, youth activists in Parkland, Florida, participated in the only countywide initiative in the United States to require all high schools, middle schools, and elementary schools to offer speech and debate. When the tragic shooting took place, they were ready to advocate for positive change.

We remain hopeful in our work because public speaking has the potential to bring us back to the deeply human endeavor that inspired us to teach in the first place—engaging learners to create a world that is more inclusive and just. Supporting learners' communication skills is hard work that involves more than a presentation at the end of a unit. It is the practice of human expression.

1

Youth Silence

Stories lift the veil on the emotional universe of youth voice. They allow us to see beyond a young person's external engagement to an internal mess of hope, doubt, effort, and regret. They remind us that youth voice is more than a survey; it is the expression of identity.

In this chapter, we focus on youth stories about what it feels like to be silenced. Rather than using research to justify youth voice, we use stories to root us in the honest reality we will never know unless we ask young people and offer them space to answer. Stories in this book are unedited, and for this chapter, the only prompt the respondents received was to tell a story about being silenced; any other choices about what they shared were completely up to them.

As you read the youth stories and poems in this chapter and through-out the book, we hope you view them as being just as significant as research and practical guidance—or more so. Don't skip them. We hope you let these young people's messages breathe and settle in your brain as you ask yourself what surprises you or what deeply resonates. By illus-trating what silence looks, feels, and sounds like from people who live it, we hope their stories set the stage for deeper conversations about what it takes to truly cultivate and center youth voice.

Meet Will

"You're up, Will," the teacher calls, indicating where I should stand to give my class presentation.

I can't help but inventory the ways in which I might embarrass myself in front of my peers. *What if I trip on the way up? Is my argument strong? Is my subject matter interesting?* I step up from my desk, notes in hand. The brightness of the classroom catches my eyes, the sun filtering in through the windows and lighting on the desks. The light buoys up my heart as I make my slow progress up to the front of the class. I take a deep breath, *You've got this*, I tell myself.

I begin to speak.

With my eyes I trace the movement of the hands, as I articulate my speech with a gentle turn of my wrist and an extension of my fingers. I judge that those hand movements are likely more distracting for my audience than they are constructive. I hide the fluttering motion of my hand in my pocket, as my posture turns inward to reflect my inner uncertainty.

I lose my spot on my notes. I swallow, and swallow again. I break through the silence with a little laugh, but fail to anticipate the spasming of my diaphragm. My eyes gently widen as the laughter becomes a thing out of my control. I am left helpless to the convulsive motion of my body, as my laughter becomes crazed. The muscle memory of speech breaks down as my confidence in myself and my speaking ability deteriorate. Natural articulation leaves me, and I have to artificially puppeteer every movement of my hand as I bring it up to mechanically silence my fit of laughter.

"So sorry about that," I apologize, as if it were a troublesome dog which had strayed outside of my control and not the uncontrolled movement of my own voice which I was apologizing for.

The metronome beat of collapse weighs over me like a blanket of sound, obstructing my hearing as tears obstruct my sight, however the presentation continues. The up-and-down motion of my jaw seems to be sluggish in contrast with my racing mind. The words which leave my lips do not register on my ear, and I don't know anything else to do than to progress through the motions of speech. The gentle raise and lower of my soft palate and the snaking motion of my tongue manipulate my oral cavity. They transform my voice as it emerges as a drone from the back of my throat, carrying me through to the end of my presentation.

To the empty applause of my classmates, I wind my way back to my desk, my eyes fixed on the floor. As I sit down, a solemn weight of tiredness descends with me. I close my eyes and breathe deeply as I focus my energy on the intake of air, then I let out a sigh of relief. *Finished*, I tell myself.

—Will Flowers, 17

Youth Voice Is Emotional

On the outside, Will Flowers is a confident speaker. As a member of the Junior Board of The Practice Space and president of his school's speech and debate team, he is a go-to mentor and the kind of leader that anyone would instinctively trust to approach any situation with grace and confidence. When asked to describe an experience related to speaking in class, however, Will tells a story that depicts an inner image of a self-conscious, panicked teen—an image that we never see from him but that reflects how most of us would feel in his situation.

Although some of us can hide our true emotions until we collapse in relief away from judgment, the struggle reveals itself in our fiddling hands, shaky voices, and darting eyes. Struggle shows up in our empty chairs when we decide to stay home or when it looks like we aren't trying hard enough. In a world that aggressively tells us to "be yourself," "speak louder," and "conquer your fears," it is hard not to feel alone in these struggles. We learn personal doubt has no place in public speaking, and yet it still dominates and silences our willingness to talk about our experiences. Speaking in public is exhausting, but talking about that exhaustion is to admit fault.

Meet Everett

So many times throughout my life, I've felt like my voice was silent. And at times, I overlooked the places where my voice would be heard, afraid that I'd say something "dumb." I did everything I could to avoid speaking my thoughts in front of people. This continued for years. I was the kid in class who sat down, quietly did their work, and barely talked to people other than the teacher. Those were quieter times, that's for sure.

I think the one thing that made such an impact on me was being diagnosed late with Autism. Of course, just because I wasn't diagnosed didn't mean I wasn't autistic. My brain still worked differently. But I didn't know that. Because of that, I felt so out of place, my emotions were brushed aside, my opinions unheard. I didn't want to talk at all, because then, I might be able to fit in. Because when I spoke, I felt like I never did. Back then it was, and still is, something that made me wonder, "What would my life be like if I was diagnosed earlier?" and, "What if I was never diagnosed?" But if those things did happen, "I" would not be me. Whether I like it or not, all the little details that have happened throughout my life, good and bad, make me who I am. To make even a small change would create someone else. And I'm just fine with who I am now. No, I'm *proud* of who I am now.

Back when I was in second, third grade, I didn't have many friends. And a lot of them were "fake". I'd do anything they asked, even if it got me in trouble, and didn't think twice. Long story short, one day those "friends" asked me to get a ball from a roof, so I scaled a shipping container, and tossed it down. Apparently, they had run off to get me in trouble with my parents. Or maybe they wanted me to be safe. I still don't know. At that moment, already while I felt that my voice wasn't heard by nearly anyone, I didn't even think my "friends" cared. That had me down longer than it probably should have, but it really hit me hard. It made me feel like, well, garbage. And I hated myself.

Now, while it sucked, I'm kind of glad that that happened to me. Because it helped me to stop blindly following people, and helped me find who I am. While so many things have contributed to who I am today, those moments where I doubted myself, where I felt worthless? They've instead shown me the power in a voice, and the importance of a story. And that's the thing I will teach others. Instead of years passing where you feel like your voice doesn't matter, I want to make people feel that their voice is heard. Because it is. And if it isn't heard? It will be.

—Everett Aishiteru, 15

Feeling Out of Place Is Silencing

Young people are constantly picking up on clues about whether their full identities will be welcomed when they speak. When faced with quiet students in class, adults often ask, "How can I get them to talk?" Youth ask a different question: "Is this a place where I can be me?" Participation and classroom engagement are surface-level indicators of a bigger story about what it takes for young people to feel accepted by people who matter to them. Instead of thinking of quiet, well-behaved students as a good thing, we should ask, are they quiet because they are focused on learning or because they are afraid of making a mistake or feel disconnected from the content or their peers? When students seem rowdy or sullen, is it because they feel like making trouble or because they want to be noticed or hide from potential embarrassment? Voices can be silenced when people feel out of place, ashamed, or worried about saying something "dumb."

The picture becomes even more complicated when we layer on intersecting identities such as disability and gender or past experiences with peers, teachers, or public figures. It becomes increasingly difficult for people to tell themselves "This time will be different" if they have had too many negative experiences, too many painful memories, and too many times when they could not feel proud of who they are. Disrupting patterns of silencing requires young people to take risks, so they need spaces where they can feel comfortable enough to face their self-doubt and learn that their voices are powerful.

Meet Eva

Ever since I was young, I have always had a hard time speaking up for myself. Mainly because I never thought it was a good Idea. But not speaking up for myself got me into some difficult situations. In elementary school, I would get bullied often, and it became so bad to the point where I had to switch schools in the 4th grade. As I entered middle school I realized how important it was to speak for oneself. But even then I was afraid of the consequences of speaking my mind. But as I entered my first year of high school that is when I really started speaking my mind.

Being a Latina is tough. Especially when there are people around you, who don't want you here because you look a little bit different. Fortunately, I have never been directly confronted for looking a certain way, for looking a little bit darker than another person, but during the campaigning for the new president in 2020, which was between Trump and Biden, hearing a public figure (Trump) talk very negatively about my own race was painful. Hearing someone call my race and seeing us as nothing more than drug dealers, thugs, and illegals, because I'm Mexican, really struck a nerve. But what really bothered me, is how he talked about us Latinos as a whole. No matter what race it is, there is always going to be a bad apple or two. But someone's actions shouldn't be defined by race, but by who they are as a person. One person's screw up, shouldn't be another's. This isn't even about political parties, though, or who's on who's side, but about how a human treats another human. Because of things like this, I knew that it was time to speak up, and voice my opinion.

One thing that really boosted my confidence and courage to speak up for myself was seeking advice from my parents. Yes, that seems like such a hackneyed way of finding solutions for things, but my parents are a big help. My parents were able to help me with my difficulty of speaking up for myself because they went through the same thing I'm going through now. And they taught me values that I still use and live by 'till this day. Another thing that really helped boost my confidence was joining the leadership program at the Practice Space. I was nervous about joining at first because I didn't think my ideas on how to make the world a better place were valid. But when I got accepted, it really changed my life. I got to use my ideas and voice to make a podcast called "Vision Z" with my partner, on how we can help the environment from the impacts of climate change.

Because of all these things, I have grown so much when it comes to speaking up for myself and others. Now it's all I want to do. I may be Latina, but that's not my weakness. That's my greatest strength. But either way, I'm going to make a difference in this world. And for the better.

—Eva Pelayo, 16

The Importance of Self-Belief

The "stuff" of public speaking tends to dominate how we prepare young people to speak. Even for us at The Practice Space, it is easy to jump to what we want youth to talk about, so we shortchange the most important conversation: How can they build their belief in their voice? Classrooms should serve as antidotes to self-doubt. Youth need the chance to process the negative events they see and experience. Even when we don't have time to facilitate this process, they are always drawing their own conclusions about self-worth.

In the face of negative experiences that threaten their confidence and belief, young leaders like Eva notice when they are in environments that encourage and foster their leadership. Being called a leader and being given the chance to develop a leadership identity are prerequisites to participating in leadership activities and developing leadership skills. We have to question implicit biases about who is invited to participate, lead, and speak. Young people who feel lost, overlooked, or unable to organize their thoughts and actions may not initially present themselves like leaders, but they can one day become some of the most empathetic advocates for people who feel silenced or powerless. Ripple effects emanate when we help young people feel worthy of calling themselves public speakers.

Meet Cole

I was always a shy kid. I never really had a lot of friends, but I was happy in Edmonton, Alberta. I both swam and did martial arts and was a happy kid. And then I moved to California one day. I had barely any warning and knew no one other than my own family. I was on my own and had very little to no friends at the time. The cultural atmosphere was so different from that of Canada; it felt as if I was on a completely different planet. I had one thing though that did help me, and that was swimming. I was on a swim team for a significant amount of time in Canada, and finding one in California was quite easy. I wasn't able to find a martial arts studio that easily and I later found one, but much later. I was content exercising and talking to my friends on the swimming team, but it didn't work out for long.

I went to school in a small primary and middle school when I moved to California and didn't really talk to my classmates because I didn't know how to communicate well. My parents recognized this and I was introduced to The Practice Space summer camp. There, I developed my self-confidence and I learned about my love for Oratory, specifically debate and teaching. I then started talking more with my classmates and became very close friends with all of them. Through AnnMarie's help at The Practice Space, my opportunities have expanded. My grades have drastically improved and I am on the advanced honor roll at my high school. I even have a job teaching martial arts and all of those things would not have been possible if it were not for the confidence-building skills that The Practice Space has given me, specifically through the encouragement to become a better speaker. Becoming a more comfortable speaker made life easier and I felt wanted and appreciated there.

At school, there wasn't that much of an encouragement to become self-confident, but The Practice Space gave me a reason to pursue becoming a better person. My favorite experience with The Practice Space was the 2018 showcase where I performed an oratorical interpretation of Carl Sagan's speech 'On Nuclear Disarmament'. I remember it quite vividly, with black pants, a bright red shirt, and passion in my voice. The memory of speaking is quite hazy, but the thunder of cheers and applause afterwards is something I will never forget. And all of this because I was able to finally see the fruits of my efforts towards becoming a better speaker. Since then, I have joined my high school debate program, competed in tournaments, and have volunteered at The Practice Space, teaching younger kids how to debate. I have since then participated in Practice Space programs for over four years now. Finding my voice was a journey, not a destination, and I feel this was only possible by becoming a part of The Practice Space Family.

—Cole Guimaraes, 16

Positive Memories Make a Difference

In many ways, it was easier for us to help a young person like Cole develop self-confidence outside school at The Practice Space than it would have been in a school setting. We have smaller classes, the luxury of time to focus entirely on public speaking and leadership, and intergenerational mentorship from peers and coaches. It can be difficult for young people to develop their self-confidence within the walls of a classroom, but given the direct implications for their participation, effort, and dreams, we should do everything possible to support that development. Cole's story highlights the fact that building self-confidence is a journey, and it is important to embark on that journey feeling like part of a family. Beyond a sense of safety and community, it helps to have positive memories of public speaking that can combat future moments of struggle. Positive memories help a young person say, "My voice is worth it, no matter what else I might face."

The older you get, the harder it is to take risks. The stakes get higher, and people expect you to know more. Without the ability to reflect on past experiences and the language to express your identity, it is easy to let fear silence you. In our work across grade levels, we are often reminded that elementary school students are capable of performing public speaking tasks similar to those undertaken by middle and high school students because they can be more fearless. Helping them speak effectively requires a bit of structure, clarity around expectations, support with teamwork, and simplified language in directions and prompts. In contrast, older youth need our support in taking risks, making choices, reflecting on past experiences, and finding the words to describe how they feel. They need to see examples of people speaking up and hear contrasting perspectives and different sides of an issue. They need to feel that they are allowed to change their minds and make mistakes. The end goal of speaking publicly should go beyond getting a good grade. Young people should be able to assert themselves unapologetically for who they are and to feel capable, cared for, and free.

Meet G

I first heard the word 'queer' (in the context of identity) when my high school's GSA (Gay-Straight Alliance) became QSA (Queer-Straight Alliance); at the time, I identified as an ally to LGBTQ individuals. High school was overwhelming, and I was probably scared of feeling even more alienated from the majority of my classmates. I also identified as cis-gender, or a person whose gender corresponds with their birth sex. I figured I wasn't trans because I did not want to be a 'man,' and unconsciously suppressed deeper exploration of my gender. Now, after years of learning to honor all parts of myself, I identify as non-binary and use they/them pronouns.

But how did I get here? As someone assigned femininity at birth, my body and my choices have always been criticized. I was told to wear longer shorts and less makeup, and felt ashamed of wanting to be perceived as attractive. I was given birth control methods instead of personal anecdotes about intimacy, and felt stifled in communicating the joy I experienced with other bodies. These struggles are modest compared with folks who face rampant homophobia and transphobia on a daily basis, but still consequential. While in college, I was privileged to be surrounded by loving communities who helped me explore myself through language and fashion. I stopped worrying about fitting perfectly into labels. I cut off my hair and felt freer than ever to wear dresses. I began noticing more than ever how pervasive gender is in everyday speech and actions.

Many of my friends and family had to put in time and energy to readjust how they spoke about me. I tried to encourage questions, avoided asking for apologies, and checked in to make sure people were comfortable with being corrected. I appreciated when people introduced themselves with their pronouns, or accepted 'they' in addition to 'she/he.' I found classrooms where teachers normalized including pronouns with introductions to be welcoming and affirming. When people struggled with changing their language after years of conditioning, I suggested that instead of using any pronouns, they use only my name.

At the end of the day, I am simply me. I am trying to live as authentically and unaffected by society's expectations as possible. I am trying to validate all forms of expression and joy. I believe wholeheartedly that if we work to uplift each other, despite our differences, we will all grow and thrive.

−Genevieve Simmons, 25

The Goal: Feeling Affirmed, Feeling Free

It is not an accident that when asked to tell a story about being silenced, young people in this chapter told stories about their identities and the emotional journey of developing them. Their stories reveal the complexity of intersectional identities that are always in motion and the importance of finding the language and confidence to express them. Incredible agency and hope can emerge from hurt and confusion. The activism of young people must be respected instead of infantilized.

As educators, we can use public speaking as a tangible way to explore the intangible nature of identity, silence, and freedom of voice. For young people to develop the power of their voice, they need to believe that it is OK to be who they are and feel equipped with the self-awareness and techniques they need to assert, question, and reassert their ever-evolving sense of self. They need to know that feeling like an imposter is not the result of something being wrong with them. Instead of conquering fears or ignoring their existence, young people need to be able to name sources of silencing and express their complex experiences if they are ever going to feel free. Avoiding topics like grief, loneliness, or alienation because they are too "adult" is not the answer, and we cannot undercut the authentic feelings of young people to preserve our own comfort. It is a deeply uncomfortable journey for everyone, and we cannot pretend that it's not.

2

Brave Spaces to Combat Marginalization

A classroom should be a place where everyone feels safe and affirmed. As in any social context, the safety of classroom culture depends on people's words, actions, motivations, and attitudes. Without intentionally cultivating equitable conditions and disrupting harmful patterns of behavior, we end up with classrooms where young people are afraid to speak and cannot be themselves, or where only some voices matter and others are marginalized (even when our intentions are honorable). When this happens, voices are not only silenced, but young people are blamed and punished for not trying hard enough, not being outgoing enough, not *being* enough.

Research out of Stanford University defines *identity-safe classrooms* as environments where student experiences and backgrounds are valued and students "believe that their social identity is an asset, rather than a barrier to success in the classroom, and that they are welcomed, supported, and valued" (Steele & Cohn-Vargas, 2013, p. 5). Combating marginalization in the classroom relies on the equity literacy of teachers, who should be on high alert, making sure inequities do not go unchecked and proactively promoting identity safety (Cohn-Vargas et al., 2021). According to Stanford researchers, "Teachers create a sense of belonging when they are conscious of group dynamics and intervene when necessary. A classroom can become a safe home base for the students . . . and support for students' sense of belonging must be upheld in practice" (Steele & Cohn-Vargas, 2013, p. 135).

Approaches to creating identity-safe classrooms must also go beyond teacher-directed action; teachers cannot be the sole bearers of the responsibility to keep young people safe. Identity safety cannot thrive amid gotcha tactics from adults trying to reinforce "good" behavior or schools hyper-focused on getting young people to comply, behave, and fit into a measurable mold at the expense of their identity. Identity safety requires a holistic approach in collaboration with young people and their families to "encompass the sense that who you are matters. In an identity-safe environment, you are not invisible and do not have to leave part of yourself at the door to feel a sense of belonging. You can be yourself, just the way you are, and thrive in the world" (Cohn-Vargas et al., 2021, p. 3).

The voices of youth and the development and education of those voices play an essential role in identity safety by transforming classrooms into simultaneously safe and brave spaces for youth expression. For Sheila Mckinney, who at age 16 was named the first youth poet laureate from Richmond, California,

A safe space is a space where you can come and connect with everybody and share the same experience. A brave space is where you are out of your comfort zone and where you are doing things that you normally don't do. They're both good, sometimes you need to come out of your comfort zone to know and learn more about yourself.

This chapter will continue to draw on interviews and poems of two Black women, poet Sheila Mckinney and her teacher and debate coach, Michele Lamons-Raiford.

imagination classroom

when my big toe
touches the school campus
i fall in love with it
again
and again
and again
every time

the welcoming energy that i look forward to
Posters on the walls that I can relate to
Corny gifs
Smiles that warm hearts
I wish this existed

leaning on anybody here
is like leaning on a brick wall
the adults here don't just hear you
they listen
they don't judge you
they understand
they don't make you feel less than
because you think different
or act different
or sound different
mistakes are talked about
instead of punished
Here lies
loyalty
honesty
love
comfort
equity
equality

Thousands of activities
diverse education
life skills
Things that actually bring me the desire to excel
intelligence reflecting work ethic
which means my generation would have all A's
paid internships and positions

green vegetables
clean water
no cavity encouraged items

oat milk
homemade burgers
rice that looks so good
each piece makes my mouth water
cafeterias where kids perform their talents
while others eat and enjoy the show
if only we could come to realize
this is how it's supposed to go

the mind of every young person
coming together to make our home
our home
the ability to express myself with clothes
no you can't put me in a box
i don't fit in
in this version that's not allowed

teachers like second parents
a trust so engraved
i never have to wonder why im here
these humans right here will be the reason there's no dropouts
no systematic oppression
they have the power to eliminate
any wrongdoing when it comes to
teaching generations
this is peace within the school community

—Sheila Mckinney, 16

The Goal: Full Expression of Identity

Identity safety is more than an academic idea; it is a powerfully positive emotion. It is a state in which you are unencumbered by the weight of societal expectations and oppressive histories, and you can act on the urge to share your story without fearing it does not matter. You can retain the same joy you felt during show-and-tell in preschool, when you could barely contain the excitement to share parts of your life because you felt proud of who you were.

The goal of identity safety is expression that stems from the knowledge that people will listen, learn, and help one another along the path to making choices about the future. The road to full expression and joy is not the same for everyone. As Bettina Love, who coined the term *abolitionist teaching* in her 2019 book *We Want to Do More Than Survive*, mentions,

> There is joy and then there is Black joy. Both are necessary for justice; however, Black joy is often misunderstood. Black joy is to embrace your full humanity, as the world tells you that you are disposable and that you do not matter. Black joy is a celebration of taking back your identity as a person of color and signaling to the world that your darkness is what makes you strong and beautiful. Black joy is finding your homeplace and creating homeplaces for others. Black joy is understanding and recognizing that as a dark person you come with grit and zest because you come from survivors who pushed their bodies and minds to the limits for you to one day thrive. (p. 120)

We live in a world with a multitude of threats to self-expression and stark divides between who feels entitled to voice their beliefs and who faces danger every time they open their lips. Legal scholar Kimberlé Crenshaw coined the term *intersectionality* in 1989 to describe how all forms of oppression intersect and should be considered at those intersections. As she explains, identities are too often erased at the intersection of race and gender (as in domestic violence narratives), and self-expression is an important tool for engaging in dialogue, being able to explain and defend thinking, and advocating for needs. Cultivating both safety and bravery for young people to speak publicly begins with naming the barriers and threats to their identities.

Creative self-expression is also how young people handle trauma. According to medical professor Lisa Najavits (2019),

> One way to cope from trauma is creativity. Creativity allows you to convert emotional pain into authentic expressions of your truth that inspire others or contribute to the world. Creativity can occur through traditional arts such as painting, writing, and theater; and

broadly, through intellectual work, spiritual pursuit, or a social justice mission. (p. 40)

Threats to Voicing Identity in Schools

Oppression can still happen even when we have the best intentions and even when we are trying not to silence young people. One of the biggest barriers occurs when young people are taught to believe that their life experiences are somehow unimportant, unworthy, or wrong. We need to intervene when we witness young people starting to internalize the idea that their voices are not important, or when they begin to learn that some voices are more important than others. Experiences that "instruct us in our own inferiority" (Illich, 1971, p. 29) can happen when we hear these messages directly, when we see people who share our views being mistreated, when we witness body language that disregards our presence, and when we can just sense that we aren't valued. In 1903, W. E. B. Du Bois described this shadowy feeling of being a problem as "measuring one's soul by the tape of a world that looks on in amused contempt and pity" (p. 5). If expression is how we communicate our identities but only some types and styles of expression are welcomed, then not every identity is valued.

Public speaking is a concrete place to start such discussions because traditionally accepted public speaking norms are often a microcosm of a world full of prejudice and stereotypes. We need to notice the difference between speakers who choose to use techniques to explicitly connect with their audience and speakers who imitate everyone else because they want to avoid negative consequences. Together with young people, we should ask the following questions:

- What is "good" public speaking? What has influenced this definition?
- Why do public speakers always have to be loud?
- Why is expressing uncertainty (e.g., saying "um") frowned upon?
- Why is it so hard to be vulnerable?
- Why does public speaking always have to fit a particular mold, whether it be topic, style, tone, or structure?

- Where do nerves, anxieties, and discomfort related to public speaking come from? Why are some people excited to speak, while others are crippled by fear?

Through discussions that explicitly name barriers to public speaking, young people and educators alike can strengthen their awareness of the conditions surrounding expression and voice. According to Sheila Mckinney's high school teacher and coach, Michele Lamons-Raiford, "The purposeful dismantling of silencing can become a ripple effect in your classroom. Sometimes, you just have to spark that flame." Educator-researchers Mirko Chardin and Katie Novak (2021) concur in their book *Equity by Design*:

> We need to normalize discussing and addressing issues that typically make us uncomfortable: privilege, race, class, gender identity, religion, sexual identity, and ability. We must embrace the fact that our classrooms and school need to be brave spaces in order to truly be transformative. Brave spaces are ones in which we have the courage to lean into discomfort for the sake of authentic conversation, dialogue, and practice. The desire to maintain a sense of comfort, while addressing issues of inequity, reflects privilege, which can easily be surfaced by asking whose level of comfort we are concerned with: Is it that of our students who have been disabled by the system and our practices, or is it that of our own? (p. 10)

Rather than pretending that public speaking is an innate talent independent of external forces, we need to recognize that who gets to speak and how they are expected to speak is both a product of history and a modern-day force for determining value and worth. Public speaking is too often an indicator that stereotypes, fear, and oppression are still active and very much alive.

Systemic Silencing

When people have been oppressed and systematically silenced, voicing their identity is in itself an act of resistance. More than resistance, young people should also be taught that they can use their voices to thrive, live, and express joy. When they speak and participate, young people want to be valued and accepted, as they should be. Unfortunately, this is not the default in an education system where Black girls are suspended at a rate that is six times higher than that of their white female peers, darker-skinned Black girls are suspended at a rate that is three times greater than that of those with lighter skin, and Black girls are branded as disruptive or defiant (as cited in Love, 2019, p. 5). In addition to the differential treatment of Black youth in classrooms across the United States, the education industry itself is built around the narrative that Black children are underserved, failing, and need to be fixed. As Bettina Love (2019) put it best:

> Creating the narrative that dark people are criminals to justify locking them up for profit is no different from continuously reminding the American public that there is an educational achievement gap while conveniently never mentioning America's role in creating the gap. . . . The barriers of racism, discrimination, concentrated poverty, and access to college—persistent, structural barriers—cannot be eradicated by tweaking the system or making adjustments. (p. 10)

When curriculum is taught without examining whose voices are being valued, young people are left to reach their own conclusions about whether their voices matter. In an interview, Sheila Mckinney said this:

> I like school, but sometimes I feel like I'm not learning what I'm supposed to. I don't want to learn about the white man and what he's accomplished, I want to learn how the past relates to me so I can move forward in the future and know what not to do and what to do.

Her teacher, Michele Lamons-Raiford, concurred:

> I think silencing comes from the curriculum. If no one ever sees themselves in the curriculum, in your assignments, your lessons, your discussions, and they can't see themselves at all, that's a form of silencing. Blindness to social and emotional health is also a form of silencing. The transition is so much bigger after the pandemic. Are we

so focused on the "catch up," the "learning loss," that we silence the social and emotional health that they need? Is there someone who is going to affirm their voice?

unspoken similarities

when that door closes while i'm sitting at my desk
i swear i can hear a jail cell close
see bars on my school windows
Feel hopeless faces around me
Look at the hard chairs
that are gonna have my back aching in 5 minutes
Officers walkin by every 3 minutes
staring at you
like they just can't wait for that referral
you get when you voice your opinion
or educate the teacher
or better yet stick up for yourself
School officials punishing by sending us away
To max
and when they see you struggling
they make you swallow more tacks
when you're called out for being unique
the reason being
the miniature box they tried to put an elephant and a lion in
would never work
The disgusting words
you used
to make us feel like we don't belong
Ahh The system
where whenever officers want to harm us they do
where the innocence is stripped away
I'm supposed to sit here and listen to the white people talk,
read me their books, and educate me on their history
when you have done nothing but made the very jail
my sisters sleep in every night

The very stereotypes that puts bullets in my brothers
the lack of education about the strange fruit
hanging from the poplar trees
infuriates me beyond belief
the system
educational or correctional institutions
can't decide
because my black and brown people have been struggling
to see the difference
they send us out in handcuffs at the school house
They suspend and expel for minor issues
sleeping
breathing
telling the truth
Standing up for our rights
but yet Becky got a warning for selling drugs
in other words they swept it under the rug because
Mommy and Daddy knows how to finesse
mommy and daddy knows how to put colored people in jail
Because they feel need to make a profit
off a human being struggling
Crimes that are often seen as justified
nothing is justifiable about a murder
Sad to say this education system looks a lot
like the corrupt legal system

—Sheila Mckinney, 16

Affirmation Instead of Silence

Affirmation is essential to creating identity-safe classrooms where youth can feel proud of their voice and their stories. To inspire pride, affirmation must be genuine. For young people and adults alike, affirming someone's voice is not genuine if we still believe that we know best, or if we are just going through the motions and being performative by saying they did a "good job." It is not affirming to be thrown empty compliments or to clearly realize that someone has not truly set aside their own biases, even while they say nice things. We cannot be genuine without examining our own privilege and reflecting on why it is hard for us to understand or empathize with someone's words, or why we think someone's remarks aren't "good." Is it because the remarks lack clarity and focus? Or is it actually because the way the person chooses to communicate does not align with our past experiences and assumptions about how people should speak? To be genuine, all listeners must constantly examine these questions.

Affirming the voices of young people means meeting them where they are and teaching them how to effectively communicate their thoughts and experiences in settings that matter to them. Offering rigorously specific and practical guidance means understanding speakers' intent and helping them realize that vision on their own terms, in their own contexts. Young people feel seen when we have enough knowledge about what they are trying to say and where, and when we believe in them enough to care about helping them communicate their ideas (rather than judging them for their work in progress). As Michele Lamons-Raiford confirms:

> The affirmation of language means teaching people how to use their voice in different venues, in different situations, with family, friends, and in jobs. You don't have to lose your voice just because you are changing how you say something. Know your room, know your audience, say your message in different ways. The ideal classroom to affirm youth voice would be figuring out what voice means to each one of them and providing different avenues and outlets for them. Affirmation means saying: your voice is so powerful that it can break molds.

From a young person's perspective, Sheila Mckinney relates:

> Life skills should look like how to express yourself, some people don't know how to do that. I don't just mean expression, but creative expression. I use my poetry to highlight Black Women, and I want to highlight what we go through and the adultification of Black girls, the

school to prison pipeline, the sexual assault to prison pipeline. My poetry, I want it to be around youth power, police brutality, and the different places I consider home, like my brain, my skin. Everybody has something to put on the table. Those who don't know how to put something on the table need help in areas like expressing themselves or coming to realize they have talent.

Reflecting and Being Well

Young people can sense how people feel about them and whether they fit the mold of success. Before getting out lesson plans and classroom shopping lists, creating identity-safe classrooms where every young person feels brave enough to speak means stopping to reflect. Young people can only express their full selves if they feel like they will be accepted for who they are. As educators, we need to regularly reflect on our capacity for acceptance. Here are some ways to do that:

- **Reflect on your school environment.** What narratives drive success in your school? What is the profile of someone who succeeds? What is the profile of someone who doesn't? Are these categories fixed or flexible?
- **Put yourself in a young person's shoes.** What is scary about school? What moments do they look forward to in school and what do they dread? How does this vary for different people, based on their history in school?
- **Examine your biases.** Do you know (and actually love) all young people? Who are you drawn to and who do you listen to most? Who do you avoid or dread? Where do these reactions come from? How do you treat individuals differently?
- **Dig deep in yourself.** Do you even have the head space to think about these questions? Or are you so tired and exhausted that you just have to go through the motions? Are you in freedom mode—focused on the pursuit of educational freedom for every young person—or are you in survival mode?

Creating spaces where young people have a voice takes a lot of energy, especially when it comes to deep and active listening. It is easy to listen for the "right" answer and much harder to listen for how a person thinks or feels. Youth voices should not be empty vessels that recite and parrot what we expect them to say; instead, their voices should express how they are human, who they are becoming, and how they are forming ideas about themselves and the world. Their emotional well-being and health need to be at the center of any space that values their voices. At the same time, as Bettina Love (2019) reminds us:

> For schools to be well, educators need to be well. Educators need free therapy, love, compassion, and healing, and to embrace theories that explain why getting well is so hard. Teacher wellness is critical to creating schools that protect students' potential and function as their homeplace. Educators, students, and parents need to be on a path to wellness together for schools to be sites of healing. Schools cannot be doing just alright; they have to be well by putting everyone's mental health as the first priority and understanding how systems of oppression spirit-murder children. (p. 161)

Universally Designed Planning

It takes a great deal of planning to ensure that every young person can have a voice in your classroom. Increasing access to expression and voice involves providing tools and entry points that eliminate barriers. This approach is a core part of a framework and set of accessibility guidelines known as Universal Design for Learning (UDL), which was created by the research center CAST with what it describes as "a singular ambition: bust the barriers to learning that millions of people experience every day" (CAST, n.d.). As a planning tool, UDL draws upon cognitive neuroscience research that explains how three networks of the brain—recognition, strategic, and affective—work together to shape how learners take in information, express knowledge, and motivate themselves. As learners participate in classroom learning, they can encounter barriers that get in the way of their participation. The framework emphasizes the need to anticipate and address barriers to engagement (anything that prevents learners from becoming motivated and purposeful), representation (anything that prevents learners from understanding the content), and expression (anything that prevents learners from expressing their knowledge). When it comes to expression, eliminating barriers means going beyond the easy statement "We need to listen to students" and instead thinking about "How can I create the conditions where young people are excited to speak and feel welcomed when they do?"

Planning to Increase Access

Once you have reflected on your own biases, guided by the points in the earlier bulleted list, the next step is to ask yourself, "Who are the young people in my classroom, as learners and as people?" Although you may not know much about them at first, creating brave and safe spaces to speak means starting with helping them reflect about their identities, as opposed to jumping right into content. Even more important, you must continually test and revise your early answers to the "who" question as you deepen your knowledge about your class, eventually seeing them as being more than "students" and as complex, fascinating people. Here are a few additional questions to ask over time:

- What would the learners in my class talk about without me there?
- What are their hopes and dreams?
- What scares and worries them?
- What are their superpowers?

As you begin your planning process, backward mapping for youth voice involves steps that explicitly build the confidence and develop the speaking and listening skills required for young people to be able to express themselves to the fullest. Figure 2.1 summarizes the process.

Establish Go-To Daily Structures

Beyond your overall scope and sequence, brave spaces for youth voice should also involve a daily experience that is consistently clear and

---

FIGURE 2.1
Backward Mapping for Voice

Step 1: Identify the final opportunity for expression, making sure it represents a meaningful and significant accomplishment. Think about what you want to help your learners say and to whom, as opposed to being overly focused on the format of the assignment (i.e., assigning a speech for the sake of having them give a speech, as opposed to concluding that a speech is the best way to communicate their message to their audience).

Step 2: Imagine the most effective vision of that final accomplishment. List the skills involved in getting everyone to the desired end point. For example, a speech might require the ability to outline and research, along with delivery skills such as volume and hand gestures to emphasize points.

Step 3: Put the skills in order of ascending difficulty, or an order that makes sense to build up to the accomplishment. It is important for learners to start off right away with early success to get them excited and motivated.

Step 4: Figure out a task/activity that teaches, practices, and improves each skill. Decide what you will grade and what will be left ungraded. It is important to have ungraded tasks to alleviate a feeling of being judged (which can be stifling to expression-in-progress).

Step 5: Create a rough calendar of how many days you will spend on each task. As you plan, you should also consider how many days you will need for the final accomplishment.

encouraging. Reflect on how you plan to set the tone at the beginning of each class through your language and energy. Plan to begin by framing the big picture and purpose of the class, and use language that makes the learners feel important and significant, having voices that are worthy of participation. Limit the time you spend speaking at the beginning of the class (set a timer if you need to!), and get young people talking in a low-stakes way as soon as possible, bringing in their own lives through stories or personal connections to the content. Do not begin with tasks in which young people have to speak for the whole class, especially if there is a clear right answer.

In addition to a consistent plan for opening activities, it is helpful to have a regular routine for the flow of the class, including expectations for expression. Think carefully about when you should talk and when learners should talk. Whose voices would prompt the most learning, and when? What activities would elicit the most joy and imagination? Although you may need to spend some time reviewing key concepts of content, it is equally important for learners to work through their uncertainty out loud, asking questions and solving problems together. Here is an example of what a daily flow might look like:

- Start with why today's class is important, displaying your own genuine energy.
- Engage in an opening small-group or pair activity in which learners share their own personal stories or prior knowledge, or generate questions and need-to-knows together.
- Teach any key concepts or new information (limit to a third of the class time or less).
- Engage in expression tasks (e.g., discussion, group work, presentations, storytelling, debate, other formats). Offer scaffolds to help learners express themselves, including individual or pair preparation time to gather thoughts, sentence starters to help them speak on the spot, or graphic organizers to plan their remarks.
- Share out or practice speaking.
- End with a routine related to summarizing learning, synthesizing progress, or giving shout-outs to specific people for how they connected or learned from what someone said.
- Later on, regularly reflect on your lessons and ask, *Was there joy and creativity? Were learners able to express their own personal connections and use their imaginations?*

Consider the Barriers

It can be overwhelming to think about creating brave spaces to speak and learn in a world where there is so much fear. But encouraging youth expression does not mean shying away from the discomfort of speaking up. Productive struggle is important for learning. As you plan, it is important to begin by naming the barriers to expression. Some common barriers to confident communication include the following:

- **Internal barriers:** Self-doubt, struggle with self-belief, challenging emotions and stress, trauma

- **Identity barriers:** Negative or complicated experiences with school in the past
- **Content and comprehension barriers:** Struggles with language, text, prior knowledge
- **Environmental barriers:** Sight, hearing, or movement barriers and anything in the physical environment that impairs participation
- **Engagement barriers:** Lack of interest, lack of options and choices, not feeling personally connected with the people or the task

To address barriers, it can be helpful to start with a two-column table like the one in Figure 2.2. Think about a particular young person and name one specific barrier under each category, along with a strategy or accommodation that would help alleviate that barrier. Make sure you think not only about learners who noticeably struggle in class, but also those you know little about or those who consistently succeed. After thinking about an individual, try thinking about the whole class, keeping your list limited to a single barrier in each category. Although Figure 2.2 describes a hypothetical individual, we have found that in a single class, entire groups of young people encounter the same barriers, making these accommodations broadly useful.

Accommodations are not meant to be quick fixes or tweaks to classroom practice, and they should not be used to lower or significantly modify expectations. Each accommodation is only a way to begin longer-term transformation of classroom conditions by addressing specific barriers. They may not always work, so your best tool is more information and more reflections from young people on their past experiences. For instance, ask the learners in your class about their barriers to speaking up. Create a quiz, checklist, or poll about anxiety related to public speaking and how they feel about speaking up for themselves or presenting their ideas. When combined with conversations about implicit bias and questioning the origins of public speaking norms, these measures enable young people to explore how their own experiences relate to a broader context. Younger children are also capable of having these important conversations, especially if you modify language to be more concrete or add pictures and

FIGURE 2.2

Examples of Barriers and Accommodations

Individual Barrier	Accommodation Example
Internal: Easily overwhelmed by stress and trouble with breathing when speaking	Teach breath exercises and use self-affirmations to quiet self-doubt.
Identity: Past experience with a panic attack when giving a speech	Prioritize opportunities to have success giving speeches, including recording them in advance or having the option to give them seated, with notes, in the learner's primary language or from a different place in the room; gather more information to dig into deeper issues through written reflections and confidential conversations.
Content and comprehension: Topic for the speech unrelated to personal or prior knowledge	Offer options for the learner to take a different perspective on the topic or bring in voices that have been typically silenced.
Environmental: One of only a few girls in the class and only girl of Asian descent	Take care when grouping, ensuring that every group has a mixture of personalities; privately ask them if there are people they prefer working with and group them with one of those people.
Engagement: Not having many friends in the class and struggling to connect with others	Build in activities to help young people discover what they have in common and routines that encourage peers to give specific positive feedback.

colors that symbolize how they feel. For instance, asking questions about their identity in school might involve a written prompt such as this: "Do you wake up excited to go to school every day? Tell me about a time when you were excited and tell me about a time when you were not excited."

Shifting Power and Encouraging Participation

In addition to its benefits for learners, reflection is also important for you as an educator, as discussed earlier in this chapter. Although collective movements toward educator wellness are essential to cultivating youth voice, individual self-awareness is key to delivering on the promise of your plans. Know what it takes for you to be a good listener, and identify a few personal routines for centering yourself and clearing your brain, so you can see young people for who they are and not for how they are affecting your stress level. In moments of stress, it is easy to resort to coping patterns centered around controlling behavior and getting people to be quiet and comply. Encouraging expression is the opposite of demanding compliance, and such encouragement inherently releases control. It requires a clear headspace and a genuine desire to hear what young people have to say and to shift power to them.

A Closer Look at Discussion

Whole-group classroom discussion is one of the most common vehicles for youth voice and can also reflect the implicit power dynamics in the classroom. The voices of young people are stifled when they sense that those around them do not care what they really think. Participation is therefore influenced by teacher language, how questions are worded, and how people react or respond to youth contributions. Call-and-response questioning (in which the teacher asks the class to state or guess the right answer to a question) reflects a classroom dynamic where the teacher is the sole holder of power. In this context, it feels scarier for young people to speak up unless they have a history of success and being rewarded in school. Encouraging participation during discussions instead involves the following elements:

- **Open-ended language.** Use language to express that you genuinely want to know what they think and don't have a right answer in mind. If you do have a right answer in mind, you should just present it as direct instruction rather than pretend it is part of a discussion.
- **Clear questions.** Ask short, concrete questions that get right to the point. For example, after you present some new information, ask questions such as "I'm curious—what is your first reaction to hearing x?" or "What about this is confusing?" If the content is controversial, ask, "If you were on the opposite side, what would

you say?" If you find you've been talking for a while after asking the question, restate the question and pause. Embrace wait time, and do not be afraid of the silence learners need so they can think about and process the question.

- **Immediate validation.** When someone speaks, listen closely and then validate the point. Make it a rule to always respond first by saying what you heard or what you appreciated about the person's contribution, even if the answer was not exactly what you had in mind. Rather than faking a positive response, be honest and say something like "I've never thought about it that way before" or "I'm going to have to think more about that one." Even if an answer does not fit with your ideas, the learner still showed courage and offered a contribution, and that act of bravery deserves thanks.
- **Synthesis and transition.** When a lot of ideas are thrown about, a strong facilitator should stop and synthesize what has been heard so far and then transition to the next question or idea. Synthesizing what has been said helps young people catch up and can encourage participation by giving them something clear to react to, especially if they are not quite following the conversation. Clear transitions give direction and depth to the discussion, rather than letting it spiral at surface level.

Determining How It's Going

At times, it can be hard to tell how things are really going and whether the classroom environment is truly a brave and safe space for youth expression. Along the way, ask yourself questions such as these:

- Am I seeing more participation from a wide range of people? Am I starting to see more people share something about themselves, even if it is just through side comments?
- Are members of my class able to speak to anyone, not just their immediate friends?
- When I ask questions, do they start speaking right away, or do I have to get things started?

- Are there diverse ways to speak in my class, and does each person's expression look and sound a bit different from everyone else's?
- As a whole, is the energy of the class relaxed, excited, and confident? Is there laughter and noise?

As you begin to hear more from young people, you will learn more about their history and have more information for understanding them as individuals and revising any preconceived notions about their capabilities. At the same time, hearing more from learners means they will stop hiding their challenges. You should expect to hear them get discouraged, confused, or stuck, especially if you explicitly invite them to express their struggles and help them find language to do so. A brave space is one where young people can say, "I'm confused." To respond to their confusion, you will need to help them be as specific as possible about what they understood and where they got lost. Similarly, when they are discouraged, prompt them to provide contrasting examples of when they felt OK, what moment discouraged them, and what steps they can take to remedy their situation. It is also acceptable for you to move on when the timing isn't right to delve into areas of confusion or feeling stuck, as long as you revisit that confusion or carve out one-on-one time to discuss the situation.

Helping Youth Dismantle Oppression

The purpose of universally designed planning and facilitation is to disrupt the barriers, biases, and power dynamics that get in the way of youth voice. These intentional moves set up the conditions for full and free expression, and they represent the intense work it takes to explicitly welcome and invite learners' participation. Identity-safe conditions go a long way to setting up the reality that Sheila Mckinney describes:

A classroom should be somewhere students can come and talk and use their voice, where they can come and say their opinion. A classroom should be somewhere everyone feels welcome. A classroom should welcome all races, all ethnicities, all disabilities, all specialties, all talents. A classroom should educate me on my culture and educate others on my culture. A classroom should have a teacher that cares about each and every one of their students and does everything that they can to help them.

Care is core to creating brave, identity-safe classrooms. Part of caring for young people is also helping them dismantle the sources of oppression they have faced and will continue to face throughout their lives. Beyond teacher-led strategies, young people need to have the space to make sense of their identities and how they are dealing with identity conflicts and integrating the different pieces of who they are. Our role as adults is to help them ask the right questions and offer opportunities for them to make choices and play an active role in their education. As Michele Lamons-Raiford advises,

> You have to put advocacy in the students' hands. What do you want to learn? What do you want to study? What did you feel was missing from your previous classes? What do you wish you would have studied? Put the power of shaping that class into the students' hands.

Similarly, young people have power over their relationships with peers, families, and communities. Do they know how to handle conflicts with peers? Do they know how to strengthen and use their personal connections? Although much of this learning might happen outside the classroom, helping young people dismantle oppression also means offering them a facilitated classroom space to process their experiences. Academic learning should not be limited only to what is in the book. Instead, identity-safe classrooms are spaces where young people can dream, articulate what they imagine and expect from their world, and explore how they might engage their families, friends, and communities in those dreams. As Sheila Mckinney puts it,

> Teaching youth to combat marginalization is important because I don't want to live in a world where I can't be myself. It's important because I want justice for those who aren't here to get justice. Most definitely it's important because I want to live in a world where everybody is treated fairly and like a human being.

Final Takeaways

In describing abolitionist teaching, Bettina Love (2019) calls for "methods, not gimmicks" when it comes to seeing the world in a way that takes action against injustice and tears down the educational survival complex to "collectively rebuild a school system that truly loves all children and sees schools as children's homeplaces, where students are encouraged to give this world hell" (p. 102). Fighting oppression is personal work that relies on the voices of young people who have lived their lives on the margins, refuse to be invisible, and "freedom-dream" together in service of creating a just world. As she articulates:

> Dark students have to enter the classroom knowing that their full selves are celebrated. Not just their culture, language, sexuality, or current circumstances, but their entire selves, past, present, and future. Their ancestors, their family members, their friends, their religion, their music, their dress, their language, the ways they express their gender and sexuality, and their communities must all be embraced and loved. Schools must support the fullness of dark life as a way to justice. (p. 120)

Although planning and facilitation moves take you part of the way, creating brave spaces to combat marginalization goes beyond intellectual work. It takes ongoing reflection and personal change from adults who fully embrace the challenge. It takes young people who are ready to speak when the moment calls for it because they have been practicing for years throughout their schooling. It is hard work with unexpected twists and turns, but young people believe it is possible.

3

Expression-Driven Teaching

The world is unkind when it comes to learning something new or being the first to do anything. When this reality is compounded by legacies of oppression, it is a privilege when we can step outside our comfort zones. There is a stark difference between growing up never being afraid to take up space and growing up feeling like you always have to prove yourself worthy because of your skin, your family, your neighborhood, and how you are viewed by people with privilege. Taking risks means stepping into an unknown that is more dangerous for some than for others, and, as discussed in the Introduction, staying silent can be part of survival mode. Having a voice is tied to having power and value, which is hard to claim when you have so much to lose.

Educators are essential facilitators of the kindness needed to prepare young people to face this uncertainty and risk, not only within school walls, but beyond. They are creators of opportunities to try, learn, fail, and try again, stretching within the boundaries of what helps a young person productively struggle and learn, such as Vygotsky's (1978) "zone of proximal development," rather than panic and shut down. Youth voice doesn't just happen because we ask for it; it emerges from strong relationships and a culture that welcomes and inspires engagement.

So, what makes it possible to pursue a vision of young people feeling seen, heard, and ready when the moment calls for their voice? We propose *Expression-Driven Teaching* as a way to cultivate youth voices and facilitate equitable participation so that young people are prepared to speak, no matter what the future holds. This chapter will introduce Expression-Driven Teaching and public speaking formats, and discuss how centering youth voice and expression in the classroom meets both academic and social and emotional learning goals. To contextualize this information, it helps to ask yourself these questions:

- What do we want young people to be able to do, communicate, express?
- How do we help them to develop the skills and confidence to do so in various environments, with different audiences?
- How do we gauge their progress and support them in that process?
- How do we offer more and more opportunities to learn from young people?

Defining *Expression* and Other Terms

Before we dive into what Expression-Driven Teaching is, it's important to define a few key terms. Traditionally, public speaking is thought of as speaking to a large audience, often at a podium or with a microphone. However, we define *public speaking* as any form of speaking or verbal expression that involves communicating with another person, and *public speaking*, *verbal expression*, and *oral communication* are used interchangeably. We use the term *expression* to be more all-encompassing of the range of modalities for youth voice that go beyond the classic speech or presentation format and include such means as storytelling, podcasting, interviewing, conversation, and even poetry. We refer to *youth voice* as the authentic communication of youth identity, with the capacity to be developed over time to effectively express opinions, cares, feelings, needs, and experiences. It is more than a survey, testimonial, or choice about classroom activities. Regardless of the format, effective public speaking and expression should *always* do the following:

- Authentically reflect and fit the speaker's identity
- Clarify and illustrate a central message

- Use a format that suits the context for the message
- Connect to the concerns, interests, and lives of the audience
- Minimize distractions from the central message
- Assist listener understanding and engagement

Many traditional public speaking norms intend to address these elements. A web search for "public speaking tips" immediately results in reminders to "be yourself" and avoid filler words like "um" to minimize distractions. Ready-made templates serve to organize ideas. Where these norms go wrong is when they start restricting what kinds of voices are valued due to a hyperfocus on the output instead of on self-awareness. Too many times, we encounter girls as young as 7 years old who think they can't speak because they hate standing alone in front of everyone, struggle to speak loudly, or think they aren't "professional" enough. We see teens who don't say anything personal because "it isn't evidence." Expressing authentic opinions is reserved for those who are "good students," "leaders," or "senior." Questions about public speaking become all about oral delivery and less about the expression of ideas. As is often said on *The Great British Baking Show*, when someone spends more time on decoration than flavor, it becomes "style over substance."

In the classroom, rigid ideas about oral expression restrict who can participate freely and who feels like their voices are welcomed and valued. Even when educators value youth voice, young people will not share this feeling if there is no room for their voices to emerge and flourish. We acknowledge that clear norms and expectations for participation are important, and completely free expression is not always possible. But educators must avoid a reality where the *only* purposes of expression are evaluation and demonstration of understanding of academic content, and where such expression must adhere to the teacher's terms, comply and follow what everyone else is doing, and fit dominant norms of success.

To prepare young people for the world, it is important to adopt a "yes, and" approach to expression. Yes, educators must ask young people to express what they know and to demonstrate understanding of academic content, *and* we need to welcome their unique perspectives and opinions.

Yes, adults must determine topics to be discussed, *and* there should be opportunities for youth choice and leadership. Yes, educators should teach young people the dominant rules they will encounter in the world, *and* we should teach them how to break those rules.

When we do not take this "yes, and" approach, public speaking often becomes ineffective or dull, or it does not even occur because speakers become too afraid to fail. Instead, the ideal reality is the fostering of learners who can make choices, a strong culture where learners are valued, and expression that offers both evidence of learning and an illustration of the person behind that learning. Ultimately, communication should be about connection—to the speaker's audience, message, and purpose—which requires the speaker to learn and to create a distinctive style while considering context and listener needs. Speakers should not be the same as one another, because people are not the same as one another.

Expression-Driven Teaching Is Social and Emotional Learning in Action

If we want to value diversity, equity, and inclusion, we need to cultivate diverse forms of expression that reflect the diversity of young people in today's classrooms. We need diverse models of public speaking so that the next generation can imagine speaking up everywhere, not just on a stage, and can feel like they are capable of doing so. Expression-Driven Teaching is a way to facilitate the development of the communication skills and the inclusive environment required to cultivate youth voice and joy, while also creating opportunities to learn from the voices of young people. Expression-Driven Teaching is defined by *characteristics* relating to attitudes toward youth voice and the purpose behind facilitating expression. When exhibiting the characteristics of Expression-Driven Teaching, educators do the following:

- Genuinely care about youth expression, outside their own motives or academic requirements.
- Encourage and facilitate authentic, unfinished expression-in-progress, where thinking out loud is valued.

- Support youth to make choices about when and how they communicate, based on reflection and self-awareness.
- Evaluate youth expression intentionally to hold high expectations.
- Learn from youth expression and adjust their thinking based on youth voices.
- Help prepare young people to navigate an inequitable world where their voices are judged by others.

In essence, Expression-Driven Teaching treats oral expression as social and emotional learning in action, where what young people say is a window into their lived experiences. In educational settings, the process of developing these communication skills begins with the question "What knowledge needs to be expressed?" Knowledge includes academic content knowledge in addition to the prior knowledge and cultural "funds of knowledge" (González et al., 2009) that young people already possess. Rather than jumping into familiar activities and presentations, the next question should be "Why is it critical for learners to talk in this context?" In other words, think about how you would complete the sentence "I want to help create a context where young people can express what they . . . ." Throughout our work, we rely on seven primary "reasons" for youth voice and expression, consisting of what youth *know*, *think*, *see*, *feel*, *believe*, *want*, and *need*. Here are our definitions of each of these:

- **Know:** The prior knowledge, content understanding, and funds of knowledge young people possess
- **Think:** How young people are currently processing new concepts, information, moments, and events
- **See:** What young people notice and witness in the world around them through their unique lens and point of view
- **Feel:** How young people react and respond emotionally and physically to their world
- **Believe:** What young people have confidence in and trust is true
- **Want:** What young people desire or wish to be different about their situation and that of others

- **Need:** What young people require for themselves and those important to them to survive, learn, succeed, and flourish

For instance, teachers who want to kick off the school year by helping young people express what they feel might decide to incorporate personal storytelling into their "morning meetings" or "do nows." Teachers who want young people to express what they see might plan a media project in which young people record videos with peers about the issues they notice in their school. Using presentations to help young people express what they know is consistent with research in learning sciences that shows that summarizing and explaining material is one of the most effective ways to build knowledge structures, facilitate new learning and ongoing brain development, and help learners integrate and connect different pieces of information (National Academies of Sciences, Engineering, and Medicine, 2018).

Although presentations are a useful format for informative speaking, they are less conducive to conveying thoughts and feelings that are still in process. Presentations also encourage generalization and summary, which is appropriate for categorizing information but not well-suited for subjective perspectives such as how the content connects to the speaker's lived experiences. In everyday life, public speaking more often happens on the spot and in the moment, when people have to advocate for what they believe, want, and need without the assistance of notes, slides, or extensive preparation. Expression-Driven Teaching serves as an anchor for facilitating and planning relevant experiences for youth to speak, so teacher reflection is helpful (see Figure 3.1). Diversifying opportunities for youth expression begins with diversifying the reasons behind why youth are invited to speak.

Expression Formats to Drive Teaching

Fostering expression involves eliminating barriers through use of the Universal Design for Learning framework, which guides the development of flexible learning environments to inherently accommodate and embrace

---

FIGURE 3.1

Prompts for Reflecting on Expression-Driven Teaching

- Which reasons for expression (i.e., what students *know*, *think*, *see*, *feel*, *believe*, *want*, *need*) do you typically include in your class activities?
- Try it out: Think of a previous or upcoming lesson. What would you like students to express?
- Choose an Expression-Driven Teaching characteristic you would like to focus on for yourself in your teaching.
- How will you embody this behavior or way of being in your everyday teaching? Decide on one to three things you can do (e.g., embody genuinely caring about youth expression outside of academic requirements by validating nonacademic forms of expression, or sharing why expression matters to you personally).

---

learning differences. As such, we celebrate differences and design with them in mind. We should account for the fact that every learner takes in content in different ways and varies widely in terms of interests and motivation. In short, "there is not one means of action and expression that will be optimal for all learners; providing options for action and expression is essential" (CAST, n.d.).

Similarly, classrooms should offer opportunities for young people to use different public speaking formats as an opening for communicating different kinds of ideas, opinions, information, identities, and emotions. Six primary public speaking formats are well-suited to the reasons that young people speak in the classroom:

- Presentation
- Discussion and conversation
- Storytelling
- Poetry
- Debate
- Self-advocacy and advocacy

Also, it is important to keep in mind that listening is a central component of any kind of verbal communication.

Although presentation, discussion, and conversation are the formats used most frequently in the classroom, discussion-based formats privilege the voices of those who feel comfortable speaking on the spot, and presentation benefits those who thrive at the front of a room. Presentations and discussions are not bad methods; they are simply limited. A universally designed classroom expands opportunities for speaking and listening, and Expression-Driven Teaching methods can guide communication for different purposes. When we use storytelling as a method in a class or workshop, for example, we often hear participants react by saying, "I feel more connected to everyone now" or "I never realized that we have gone through so many of the same situations and feelings." In one workshop on confidence building, a young woman said, "Storytelling shows that there is power in vulnerability, where you can show a lesson you learned and invite others to do the same." Poetry can also be a powerful tool for expressing vulnerability through the creative use of language to express what we see, feel, and notice, which can also spark conversation. On the other hand, debate is more concrete, with organized and structured protocols that guide the expression of contrasting thoughts, knowledge, and beliefs. Self-advocacy explicitly encourages learners to articulate what they want and need, which is vital for navigating an inequitable world and owning the power of their voices to create positive change.

Expression-Driven Teaching Practices

Expression-Driven Teaching begins by examining the opportunities for youth voice, both in the classroom and beyond. In most classrooms, expression is reserved for formal assignments as well as conducting teamwork, making meaning from texts, and sharing thoughts with a partner (e.g., turn-and-talks). In terms of timing, moments of expression are usually inserted in between lectures as call-and-response exchanges, as presentations of new information, or as the culmination of a unit. These approaches are useful ways to monitor learning and check for understanding along the way. At the same time, expression can be deepened when young people have a chance to lead their learning or when expression builds relationships.

Opportunities for youth voice should also be designed to encourage diverse voices, so that equity can come to life in the classroom. In our work, we see a stark difference between who participates during question-and-answer types of activities and who participates in formats such as debate or storytelling. During an introductory prompt, for instance, one young person, Don, described himself as "an ambitious person." When given time to craft and share his personal story, Don related why he wanted to be the first person in his family to attend college, citing lessons learned from his mother and basketball. Although his story took time to gather and prepare, it was time well spent, especially since Don had not spoken at all during question-and-answer discussions. The depth of the window into his life and values made his effort worth the time and helped develop stronger connections with his peers. Opportunities to encourage diverse voices can also be quick as long as they are well-structured—for example, beginning a unit with a 15-minute debate, with structures for helping young people articulate different viewpoints.

The main takeaway is that these opportunities need to be intentionally designed, timed, and communicated to invite different voices to speak. This process involves four primary Expression-Driven Teaching practices: (1) facilitating relationships, (2) facilitating the fundamentals, (3) facilitating choice and agency, and (4) facilitating growth.

Teaching Practice 1: Facilitating Relationships

As discussed in Chapter 2, expression requires safety, which is cultivated when peer-to-peer and student-teacher relationships are strong. By viewing all speaking as public speaking, we also recognize that fear, anxiety, and doubt are baked into the process of communicating with others in any format. According to research from the University of Minnesota, the fear of public speaking stems from a fear of judgment, especially in the presence of uncertainty (i.e., unfamiliar audiences, content, and situations), unequal power dynamics (i.e., being positioned as "less than" due to experience, age, or background), and struggles with self-belief as a result of internalized oppression (*Communication in the Real World*, 2016). Naming and alleviating these fears is critical in Expression-Driven Teaching, and it is important to recognize that, by nature, almost everything that young people say is new and in process. Not only are their situations inherently uncertain, but also they have less power over the direction of their lives. Moments of communication in the classroom are high-stakes occurrences, both in terms of grades and the perceptions of their teacher and their peers.

There are also many parallels between teaching practices that culti-vate youth voice and other active-learning approaches such as project-based learning and social and emotional learning. At their core, these types of approaches, along with Expression-Driven Teaching, are student-centered and rooted in the philosophy of "learning by doing," and the learning environment is essential for young people to feel comfortable enough to engage in interactive learning experiences.

To establish relationships, it is first important to meet learners where they are. Doing so requires information about various aspects of their identity, including the following:

- Goals
- Histories
- Interests
- Preferences
- Triggers

Communication should always be driven by a clear goal and purpose, so we should immediately collect information about what learners want to communicate and why, and how they want to feel when they speak. In addition to documenting goals, it is always essential to gather back-ground about learners' history and experience. Have they always spoken up in class? Are they new to this country or school? Do they have a back-ground in performing, such as music, acting, or debate? Our understand-ing of individual histories should also evolve with time and rely on asking the right questions, being genuinely curious about getting to know some-one, and putting ourselves in informal situations where we can speak to young people on their terms.

Topic interests and speaking preferences are always useful to know, and we can gather this kind of information through activities such as human polls (e.g., where students line up or go to four corners indicating whether they "strongly agree" or "strongly disagree" with a prompt) or even on Zoom (e.g., "Make a silly face if you . . . ," followed by prompts on topics and speaking preferences). Questionnaires are also especially useful for learning about what triggers learner stress and anxiety. An example is our Communication Anxiety Quiz (see Resource 6 of The Practice Space's *Confidence-Building Guide* [Baines, 2020c] at www .practice-space.org/confidence-building-guide/). Referring to someone's "superpower" reframes and validates that person's strengths. Seeking superpowers are also more nuanced than giving students fixed labels such as "class clown" or "introvert." When young people view natural aspects of self as superpowers, they can intentionally lean into that quality as they improve their communication. For instance, a quiet student can be celebrated for having the superpower of being reflective. Someone who may be seen as a flat or dry communicator can instead be commended for being serious, calm, and focused.

Information about individual learners is strengthened when we genuinely value diverse, fluid identities. Too often, we gather data solely to judge young people rather than treat them like human beings we can appreciate, learn from, and better understand. Establishing and sustaining a "culture of talk" (see Resource 1 of The Practice Space's *Coaching Guide* [Baines, 2020b] at www.practice-space.org/coaching-guide for indicators of this type of culture) means bringing humanity back to education by welcoming different perspectives and feeling a sense of joy when we communicate, rather than dread. Without an environment built on relational trust, youth voice and communication will always be stifled.

Teaching Practice 2: Facilitating the Fundamentals

When learning any new skill, it is important to feel successful along the way. If too much time passes before a learner can see any improvement, the experience of learning something new can be daunting and overwhelming. Educators can promote confidence by helping young people experience small victories and success as early as possible, while continuing to challenge them and guide their development. See Resource 7

of The Practice Space's *Coaching Guide* (Baines, 2020b) at www.practice
-space.org/coaching-guide/ for more tips on early success.

Communication skills can be divided into three primary categories:
(1) content, (2) delivery, and (3) process. When we first think about public
speaking, the immediate feedback we want to provide is almost always
related to speakers' delivery. Were they animated enough? Did they use
their hands? Did their voice hold our interest and attention? Focusing
entirely on oral delivery is a bit like focusing entirely on spelling when
judging someone's writing. It might be a necessary part of helping clarify
ideas, but it is not sufficient. For something as quintessentially human as
communicating one's authentic identity and views on the world, teaching
these skills should be challenging and complex, and there is a great deal
to teach.

The content of the ideas and the speaking context should drive all
decisions about delivery. An intimate conversation about a personal story,
for instance, should warrant a seated arrangement, a quieter voice, facial
expressions that match the story content, and a less formal approach
overall. A speech advocating for substantial changes to governmental
policy might require a strong and assertive vocal tone, with gestures that
emphasize key words and points, increasing in volume and speed to build
urgency along with the content. Due to the need for speakers to adjust to
the situation and content, it is helpful to practice different public speaking formats to develop the capacity to adapt.

The Practice Space's *Storytelling Guide* (Baines, 2020f) lists various
communication skills in each of the three categories (content, delivery,
and process):

- **Content-Related Skills**
  - **Content preparation:** brainstorming, outlining, selecting con-
    tent relevant to the audience, organizing and sequencing content,
    slide design, research skills, and identifying and using credible
    sources
  - **Speech writing:** strong beginnings that capture audience atten-
    tion, strong transitions between ideas, strong endings that defini-
    tively conclude and leave the audience wanting more, summarizing

or recapping ideas, explaining complex ideas clearly, and use of compelling language and memorable phrases
- **Adaptability:** ability to be succinct and to-the-point, persuasive speech construction, story construction, spontaneous speaking and argumentation

- **Delivery-Related Skills**
  - **Voice and tone:** breath support and control, appropriate use and variation of volume, appropriate use and variation of pitch, appropriate use and variation of speed, using voice to strengthen content, and ability to avoid distracting filler phrases or words when appropriate
  - **Physicality and movement:** strong posture and stance, using gestures to highlight content, ability to balance being relaxed with being energized, appropriate use of eye contact, using facial expressions to highlight emotions, movement and use of a stage, correct use of a microphone and other sound equipment, and ability to avoid distracting movements and fiddling

- **Process-Related Skills**
  - **Interaction with others:** listening, asking clarifying questions, asking probing questions, note-taking, collaboration with others, facilitation of discussions or teamwork, adapting to different audiences, relating to others, coaching others, and providing constructive feedback
  - **Self-management:** anxiety-coping, time management, ability to be authentic (true to self, style, and beliefs), ability to be connected with the emotions behind the content, and ability to get "in the zone" and be fully focused on the material

In light of the complexity of building fundamental communication skills, less is more; so it helps to choose one or two skills per category as the focus for a class. Regardless of focus, it is important to be explicit about what a "norm" is in public speaking (e.g., confident voice, use of gestures, having a loud voice) and offer opportunities for young people to practice those qualities as well as question them. A driving question for speakers should always be *What decisions can I make regarding my words and behavior to best highlight my ideas and connect to my audience?* Helping young people know what choices are available to them (as well as inviting them to break communication norms) goes a long way toward developing their ability to be intentional about how they use their communication skills.

Teaching Practice 3: Facilitating Choice and Agency

To practice communication skills, a central teaching practice is to be explicit about how we want young people to focus their attention. The wording, selection, and process of generating speaking prompts is critical, because clear, compelling prompts go a long way to sparking interest and facilitating participation. (See further discussion in Chapter 5.)

Once learners know what they should focus on, educators play an important role in helping them identify a clear goal for what they want to say and why. Presenting young people with a prompt that asks them to speak typically results in three situations:

- They don't know what to say and need help coming up with ideas.
- They have too much to say and need help organizing and prioritizing their ideas.
- They have ideas but are afraid to speak.
- They struggle with confidence, oftentimes due to language barriers.

For many learners, it is a little bit of everything and depends entirely on the topic and the exercise; for others, speaking always comes easily, and they are the first to volunteer. The key is to recognize that preparation needs vary, so educators play a key role in helping speakers make intentional communication choices, drive their own plan and process, and increase comfort to process fear.

For learners who have trouble generating ideas, whole-group brainstorming sessions are helpful before releasing them to work on their own. Depending on the prompt, you can have a conversation about what young people already know and give concrete examples of how an assigned topic might connect to their lives, thus sparking a sense of familiarity.

Similarly, you can provide them with real-world peer examples by sharing a brief YouTube video of a young person performing a piece of poetry, engaging in debate, or giving a personally significant speech. Identifying students who can participate in a live demonstration with you (such as demonstrating a debate or having a student ask you questions as you give a model speech) works as well. These visual/auditory models help learners understand the ultimate goal. For open-ended work where learners are asked to come up with their own topics, it helps to generate a class list or a preprepared menu of choices so that the task of choosing topics is less daunting. The task can also become more approachable by asking learners questions like "What is something that makes you lose track of time?" or "What is something that makes you frustrated with the world?" as opposed to "What is your favorite topic or passion?" or "What is your opinion about?" Adding sentence frames that coincide with the questions, such as "Something that makes me lose track of time is . . ." or "Something that makes me frustrated with the world is . . ." helps jump-start that brainstorming process by giving learners a specific place to begin. Helping classmates work with each other to brainstorm—such as having one person scribe for someone else who just talks about free-form ideas— can save time and build community.

Beyond selecting topics, graphic organizers can help young people make choices about how they want to communicate their ideas. Such organizers can pose binary or yes/no questions such as "Is it useful to tell a story in this speech?" or "Will I speak softly or loudly or a little of both?" or "Which will I choose: an informative speech to teach the audience something or a persuasive speech to convince them?" The simple act of having learners reflect on their options and make intentional choices about how they plan to communicate not only helps you understand their intentions (and think about how to help them achieve them), but also helps learners practice communicating with intention. At times, it is advisable to have some guidance by outlining some clearly fixed expectations so that public speaking activities are not completely open- ended. In our work, we tend to fix elements such as length of the speech, number of points to make, and how many people are presenting together. We also establish norms such as the following, which assist listener understanding:

- **Signposting:** Listing what you are going to talk about in the speech or previewing what you are going to say next
- **Recapping:** Summarizing points at the end of a speech to reinforce audience recall
- **Transition lines:** Offering options for bridge sentences, such as "Now I'm going to move onto my next point, which is . . ."
- **Repetition:** Reiterating key points several times throughout a speech to reinforce ideas with the audience
- **Silence/Pauses:** Encouraging speakers to decide when they need breaks between ideas to let the audience process something

Throughout our work, we have found that speakers' readiness for creating strong content and making intentional communication choices varies much more by their experience with public speaking and less by their age or grade level. The ability to make decisions about speaking also goes a long way toward building speaker confidence, because it helps to feel a sense of control in uncertain situations like speaking for an audience.

Teaching Practice 4: Facilitating Growth

Facilitation is one of the most critical skills for any educator who wants to advance more equitable opportunities for youth voice in the classroom. Learning how to effectively communicate with others is a gradual, continuous developmental process that takes time, practice, and guidance. Pausing to help young people set personal communication goals and reflect on their progress over time allows them to develop a growth mindset around public speaking, as opposed to an all-or-nothing attitude that many develop (e.g., "I am just a bad public speaker"). Feedback from the teacher, peers, and even outside audience members helps them embrace the subjectivity of public speaking and build up their self-awareness of their own superpowers and what works for the audience.

Treating public speaking as a formative assessment tool (rather than solely as a summative assessment) frames expression as a way to learn and process.

Instead of jumping right to critical feedback, it is important for young people to start learning about their strengths so that they can begin developing a strong foundation. Spending significant time only on positive reinforcement also combats the natural assumption that audiences are bored or disinterested and helps build peer relationships. Practicing speaking then becomes about learning how to make choices to express what the learner wants to say really well. When feedback is specific, helpful, concrete, and actionable, it is easier for speakers to figure out any adjustments they need to make in the future. Resources 9, 10, and 11 in The Practice Space's *Coaching Guide* (Baines, 2020b) at www.practice-space.org/coaching-guide/ offer guidance about coaching speech writing and delivery and general do's and don'ts.

Facilitating growth also means that young people should begin developing a sense of what the world will be like when they communicate with others. Practicing public speaking in front of real public audiences familiarizes learners with what it feels like to speak outside the classroom. Simulations and role-play can also help them practice speaking on the spot, which is the primary way communication takes place in the world. Incorporating more public practice opportunities also opens the door to discussions such as these:

- How are my experiences, perspectives, and worldviews different from or similar to those of others? What do I say that is different from what my audience thinks? Do people care about the same things that I care about?
- Which voices have been historically valued in my various contexts? What is culturally accepted, and how does my approach align or not align with those values?
- What voices are missing from important conversations? If I can't represent the missing perspectives, how can I step back and give different people an opportunity to share? How can I respectfully

amplify different voices and perspectives? How can I call out missing perspectives without making assumptions about those perspectives?

- What is the right timing for bringing up the kinds of topics that mean the most to me? When is my audience ready to hear my ideas? When should I speak anyway, regardless of whether people are ready to hear my voice?

Young children can also have these types of discussions to build their self-awareness. Even when these discussions do not take place, children can sense when they do not fit in, and they still worry about how people think of them. It helps to give them the vocabulary to express these experiences, and sharing can make them not feel so alone. Rewording the above prompts for younger learners might look something like this:

- What do I like to talk about? Do other people like to talk about the same things?
- What do I have in common with other people?
- What is something unique about my life that very few people can talk about?
- When will I listen to different people so I can learn about their lives?
- What are my speaking superpowers? What makes my voice stand out?
- What was a moment when I felt out of place or when people were talking about things I couldn't talk about?
- What are some examples of moments when I need to speak up for myself?

It is valuable to teach young people to push back on accepted public speaking norms and to choose what feedback to incorporate and where they might question audience perceptions. Explicitly teaching them to question, critique, and push back on how people view them is teaching them an essential life skill that puts them in charge of their own learning, as opposed to always feeling like they are at the mercy of the audience or school expectations or that they are the only person who feels out of place.

What Is Possible Through Expression-Driven Teaching

Although all of these practices may feel overwhelming at first (especially when pacing guides and standardized tests put so much emphasis on breadth of content), even taking the initial steps to incorporate them into classroom practice can save time and challenge in the long run. Even more than that, Expression-Driven Teaching practices help unearth unconscious biases, center youth leadership and personal decision making, and avoid silencing diverse perspectives. When we fail to explicitly teach communication skills in everyday classroom moments (i.e., beyond just a final assignment at the end of a unit), then it is easy to fall into default behavior such as having the same people volunteer every time or always hearing from the same voices.

Benefits for Educators

When we value and cultivate the voices of young people, teaching is a whole lot more fun. Ultimately, Expression-Driven Teaching practices help you get to know your class as individuals, not just "students" you have to evaluate and keep in line. Focusing on expression can help open up ideas for meaningful classroom projects and can encourage everyone to listen and learn from one another, which strengthens classroom climate. Facilitating oral expression also makes it easier to teach writing skills, as there are close parallels when it comes to using rhetorical devices and generating and organizing ideas to be clear and engaging.

Strengthening your practice to coach young people as speakers can also help you become a stronger communicator yourself. Helping learners speak up more often puts a heavier emphasis on giving clear instructions and articulating what you value from speakers. It can be useful for young people to hear about your experiences with public speaking and learn what aspects of the activity are fun for you and what still makes you hesitant and nervous. These kinds of discussions around vulnerability help demystify public speaking and turn it into something that is deeply human and always in progress. Fears about public speaking are not something to "conquer," "dismantle," or "disrupt"; instead, they are an integral part of how we learn about ourselves and connect.

Benefits for Young People

Expression is a vehicle for equity in the classroom because it values the diversity, expertise, and funds of knowledge that young people bring to the setting. Knowing that their voices are valued enhances young people's feelings of belonging, which drives their motivation to learn and participate. Expression promotes equitable access to content knowledge by alleviating confusion and highlighting the role of communication in clarifying complex ideas. Instead of merely expecting young people to be able to respond to questions in a whole-group discussion, Expression-Driven Teaching involves preparing everyone to find the words and approach to offer their own thoughts, opinions, and emotions.

Beyond equity in the classroom, expression can help young people create more equitable worlds for themselves. Expressing their lived experiences helps them highlight what they want and need, and the ability to listen helps them develop empathy. The ability to put experiences into words means they will be able to make their lives and learning visible to others and themselves. Teaching them how to adapt to different situations prepares them for future conflicts and equips them with approaches for navigating chasms of misunderstanding or differing beliefs.

Preparing for Judgment

It is human nature to judge expression, so we need to prepare young people for this reality so they can be judged on their own terms. Whether we are conscious of it or not, we draw conclusions about people based on how they speak and act. We judge expression to form impressions about whether someone is successful, credible, or aligned with who we are and what we want.

In professional settings, people who can articulate their ideas are viewed as credible and trusted leaders, and those who struggle are judged as "junior." In classrooms, expression is openly judged, and young people receive grades based on presentations, which affect their future success and how they are perceived by peers. In our everyday lives, we form judgments to discover "Who are my people?" basing conclusions on what we hear people say and do. As Assistant Professor of Communication Elizabeth Dorrance Hall (2018) puts it, "Our brains are wired to make automatic judgments about others' behaviors so that we can move through the world without spending too much time or energy on understanding everything we see." Expression-Driven Teaching prepares young people for this reality.

Final Takeaways

Young people do not need to "find" their voice. They already have voices, but those voices need to be cultivated, encouraged, and developed so that learners do not get discouraged about their ability to speak or are silenced over time. Classroom routines, structures, and traditions bring safety to the process of learning to speak, along with self-awareness of their own strengths. If adults do not take the time to guide young people through this uncomfortable process, then fears and anxieties can easily take over. Our collective goal should be to build confidence, so that young people feel an inner strength and self-belief in what they want to say and how they want to say it. Developing a sense of security and certainty takes time, and the origins of fear are complicated. Unpacking the process of building confidence must be part of classroom life.

The following chapters each take a deep dive into one specific public speaking format, so that you have the tools and confidence to teach diverse forms of expression. After reading about Expression-Driven Teaching, check in with yourself. Which aspects of this method excite you, which are familiar, and what would be a stretch? What are your goals for expression in your class? Like writing or math, oral expression is a form of literacy that requires practice, failure, productive struggle, and time, from all learners, including teachers. It isn't enough to judge young people solely on the communication skills they already possess; they have so much to say, and their voices deserve more from the field of education.

* * * * * *

ode to that one teacher

ode to that teacher who makes teaching
both educational and comprehensible to every generation
instead of making teaching a burden
The teacher that stands up for her students
at the board meetings
ode to the teachers that say "my babies" or "my kids"
making me feel a sense of home and comfort
me holding on to the idea of dropping out until
the sight of my favorite teacher touches my eye
ode to that teacher that let me and my homegirls
kick it in their room at lunch
putting up with my crazy thoughts
and communicating when you thought I was off
Ode to those snacks you had stashed for me in the drawers of your desk
My sincerest appreciation goes out to you
for looking out for me when I wasn't at my best
You're that reminder that school is made for teachers like you
Ode to the beautiful human
that took time to get to know me
ode
to teachers
that care

—Sheila Mckinney, 16

4

Storytelling to Value Youth Identities

For as long as there has been language, there has been storytelling. Stories can pass down traditions, share teachings, celebrate cultural identities, capture how societies lived, and sustain connections. Stories are universal, and our brain is inherently wired to receive, process, and remember them.

Storytelling as an Educational Tool

Among many other things, storytelling can be a tool for communicating how young people interact with and are affected by systemic issues such as racism, classism, and transphobia. Stories give young people permission to own their identities, convictions, and ideas, and to express them out loud.

Young people cannot afford to wait for old systems to be torn down and new ones to be created. How do we as educators support their existence within systems that do not serve them? How do we begin to undo the impact of years of systemic silencing that young people have endured? What will help young people navigate the current systems and thrive in the ones we will build in the future? Stories infuse joy into classrooms while simultaneously making space to talk about diverse backgrounds, challenges, and traumas. They invite educators, along with learners, to challenge systems and harmful narratives.

Storytelling also gives young people the freedom to reveal their identities on their terms. Providing a space for young people to speak about the many ways their identities intersect is critical to fostering an equitable environment and a brave space in which to learn. Storytelling is a powerful tool to explore and express aspects of one's identity to the world. Storytelling can be used to create the context where young people talk about the reasons for expression: expressing what they know, how they think, what they see, how they feel, what they believe, what they want, or even what they need.

There are many benefits of storytelling:

- Promotes Universal Design for Learning
- Improves oral literacy and meaning making
- Communicates inner thoughts and dreams
- Builds community, friendship, connection, and trust
- Provides fun, joyful, and engaging experiences
- Supports English language learners
- Builds active listening skills
- Improves critical and creative thinking
- Makes academic content relevant
- Develops writing, organization, and brainstorming skills
- Strengthens social and emotional learning
- Inspires social justice

Equity Through Storytelling

Stories that are told publicly are most often the ones that are deemed worthy, true, or valid. A common barrier young people face when asked to tell a story about their lives is their feeling that they have nothing worthy to share. Feeling seen and validated by family, peers, school, and the media is essential for young people to believe they are ready, willing, and able to take up space and embrace who they are. The need for validation compounds the vulnerability that already exists when sharing emotions and personal experiences. Stories help learners empower their voices by owning the many layers of their identities, processing their experiences, and connecting them to people who are listening.

In a September 2021 article, Annie Neimand and colleagues reflect on the importance of expressing the many intersecting layers of one's identity: "When we don't have a narrative that tells us how to think about an issue or when the narrative is inaccurate, partial, or too abstract, we fill in the gaps, and the stories we build in our own minds can be flawed and full of biases and assumptions" (Neimand et al., 2021). Telling intersectional stories in a welcoming learning space, among peers who will see and understand them, and with an educator who is willing to help young people see more of themselves, delivers on the promise of authentic youth voice in the classroom.

This chapter explores three stories authored by young people that illustrate the ways storytelling reflects youth identity. Here is the first of those stories:

> Our education system loves to categorize people and put them into little boxes. That white people do a certain thing, while people of color do another. One that's frowned upon. We see it all the time in movies and TV shows. The preppy white girl and the Latin gang member. Nearly all the roles for Hispanic people on screen are either the maid or a gang member. This idea of us seeps into schools. It's what people see us as. And unfortunately, our education system supports it. I'm on the debate team, and there was an instance when a white girl referred to black and hispanic people as "colored." Once corrected, she apologized and seemed embarrassed. But she didn't know better. This system has failed to educate the proper terminology for people of color, and it's heartbreaking to see. This causes non-latin people to categorize us in a box. That all of us are like that. This causes bigotry. For example, Donald Trump saying that all of us are "rapists" and that all we bring is "crime." The lack of education about hispanic people is worrisome, and it brings in stereotypes that turn into bigotry. The system has failed to introduce Latin voices and Latin education into the curriculum, which in turn, these issues form into our society.

The lack of Latin representation and voices not only turns into bigotry, but for Latin people, we feel like a ghost. That we are not seen. That our only job is a maid, gang member, or a farmer. The only history we get is Cesar Chavez. That's it. Our history is not told. We don't know where we fall in school or where we belong. It's as if the curriculum has stripped away our culture. No one can hear our cries and learn our history in the place of education. The impact of us being silenced is dangerous. Why are our textbooks filled with white history? Why does our school not teach about how President William Taft went on a murderous reign over Hispanic people? Or that we had segregated schools, communities, and weren't allowed to serve on juries in America. Or that farmworkers were kidnapped, robbed, and tortured for simply existing. Or that President Nixon said "Latin America doesn't matter." To silence my people's history is to silence us today. My generation is facing the consequences of this silence when we are put into this box full of stereotypes. My generation of young hispanic people are silenced because our education system today and our education system from our parents and grandparents time has not taught people our history and has not let them hear our voices. The system has failed us, but it's time to change that. For so long we have felt like a ghost that society has put in a box, but it's time for that to change.

—Elizabeth Duarte, 16

Whose Stories Get Heard?

Elizabeth's story is a grim reminder that pop culture, news, social media, and school systems tell stories, too. Sometimes systems communicate harmful stories that can make young people, like Elizabeth, feel invisible. They are listening and internalizing these stories. Stereotypes in pop culture reinforce the stories and behaviors young people bring into schools and classrooms, forming the basis for their opinions of their peers. If we don't intentionally disrupt this situation, then these are the stories our young people will believe. These stories make those from underrepresented communities continue to feel unwelcome and unimportant.

Curriculum should represent people from all backgrounds so young people feel seen and valued through what they learn. Young people deserve to learn the history of their people in the classroom so that they can connect to the current history they are living in and creating by simply existing. Representation in curriculum matters because without it, young people feel their history is being overlooked, reinforcing intergenerational silencing.

As educators, we have the opportunity to hold space for young people to process, question, and challenge narratives that threaten their sense of identity or make them feel like part of them is welcome and another part is not. Storytelling is a catalyst for young people to discuss the untold stories, which are often relatable and connected to them by ancestry, age, or common experience. Embracing the practice of storytelling by creating rituals where stories are shared can help them talk about these issues in ways that are both emotional and academically rigorous. Consider the following story:

> I came out to my mom as lesbian two months ago. She responded that she didn't believe in happiness, but only contentment. She told me that being queer satisfies personal want, not long term success. Painful words coming from my mother, yet I'd expected it. After all, that's why queer sexuality is so stigmatized.
>
> Throughout primary school, I often heard jargon associated with that idea of success. A big house, a husband happily married to his loving wife. That seemed to be the flashing standard wherever I looked. Deviance from that standard was shamed. Boys derogatorily calling other boys gay in primary school is certainly not an uncommon experience. Queercoded characters in popular school films shamed queer identity and flamboyancy. Teachers did nothing about it. I learned nothing about being queer from school. Queer people were talked about as other. Distant. Nonconformist in the narrative of what my future should be. That's why it took me so long to realize who I was. It's why I wished that I wasn't gay for so long. And it's why I still sometimes am scared of what my future holds.

Not one adult has ever directly told me that it was okay to be queer. My education never included my identity. And school culture never fostered inclusivity. No one ever stood up when something wrong was said about queer identity, and no one told me that I was allowed to dream of a future where I was happy outside of the confines of the heteronormative box. Knowledge is power. Any kid could be queer. And everyone deserves an opportunity to question who they are.

The Need for Stories to Be Accepted

This story illustrates that young people are always listening, noticing, and internalizing societal expectations. In fact, the messages and stories we offer them about what is acceptable are often coded and implied. Young people should not feel that their dreams have limits because only some aspects of their identities are accepted. Understanding the many layered nuances of identity is a crucial aspect of learning. Young people need the opportunity to question themselves in spaces that are safe and designed for learning on the path to deeper understanding. This is a central aspect of what is needed to achieve personal liberation. For young people, incorporating storytelling as part of learning means having choice in naming who they are, owning those parts of themselves out loud, and being witnessed by their peers and teachers. Connections deepen when young people know what it means and what it feels like to truly be seen. The following story is another example of the power of storytelling to help young people understand—and accept—their complex identities:

Sometimes I stand in front of my mirror, tracing the features of my face with my eyes. I can't help but notice how unusual those features are, how my Filipino and European genes meshed in a way that makes me look neither Filipino nor European.

I take pride in my heritage, but at times I feel as though I can't fully appreciate the history of either side. I've been on the receiving end of "you're not Filipino enough" or "you're not white enough," and though

I know words aren't supposed to hurt, they cut like a knife. It makes me feel as though my feelings towards issues revolving around my heritage aren't valid.

Sometimes, I wonder if I'm even allowed to be proud of my Filipino heritage because I'm mixed. When I was in elementary school, I used to just tell people that I am Italian-German-Irish because it was easier than explaining that my mother is Filipino. It was easier than listening to ignorant comments. Most of all, it was easier than thinking about my heritage, both of my families' histories, and where I fit into it all.

These feelings become even harder to address when I think about how underrepresented Filipinos have been in American history. Our stories as immigrants and activists have been buried and forgotten, and while there are many Filipinos in the U.S., our culture has been abandoned out of fear of racism.

However, throughout all of these feelings, I have learned to take pride in my heritage by educating myself on Filipino-American history. Although there is a lack of representation for Filipinos in history books and media, I can still show my solidarity for my community by reading about the amazing Filipinos who have so many stories to tell and so much to teach the world.

Even though there are times when I question myself as a Filipino, I am proud to be one. I am proud of my Lolo and Lola for overcoming their struggles as immigrants and as people of color. I am proud of my mother, who gives voices to Filipino Americans through her writing. I know my insecurities about this will likely never go away, but when I look in the mirror, I look at those unusual features with acceptance, knowing that those features came from generations of beautiful stories that matter.

Storytelling and Intersectionality

This story demonstrates how young people of mixed race and ancestry carry a unique intersectional burden when expressing identity. Harmful narratives are reinforced when young people spend hours a day in spaces where adults unconsciously categorize them, do not bother to learn proper pronunciation of names, or do not take time to understand their layers of heritage and ancestry. To be good stewards of learning, we can take steps to gather more complete information about young people and actively question the ways youth are systemically categorized as part of the effort for education to be "data-driven."

Young people should not feel unsure about whether they are allowed to feel pride in their ancestry. It is harmful for them to buy into the idea that there is some entity or body that bestows permission to feel like a part of a group. Instead, intersectionality asks people to examine how different sources of pride and oppression intersect to shape someone's life.

Communicating complex experiences can also be challenging across generations, because history and context play an important role. It is important (although challenging) for young people to be able to articulate how societal forces shape identity in the current day and how those identities may differ from those of 20 years ago. Knowing how to respond when faced with assumptions, biases, and rejection from people who do not understand them is also valuable for healing.

Classrooms should not be spaces where young people ignore entire aspects of what makes them who they are for the sake of accommodating a dominant culture or to spare themselves the hurt that accompanies an ignorant comment from a peer or teacher. Stories can be a powerful source of validation. When young people openly explore the complexities of their intersecting identities, they can openly own, embrace, and feel pride in the full range of who they are. Educators can combat and disrupt those constant questions that young people of mixed heritage feel obligated to answer, like "What are you?" by creating spaces that ask better questions, rooted in curiosity not category. Here are some examples of such questions:

- Who are you?
- Who are your people?
- How do you honor who you are?
- How can we help you honor who you are?
- How do you want to show up in the world?

Getting Started

In life, storytelling usually happens organically when we are with our friends or loved ones. So what does storytelling look, feel, and sound like in the classroom? Above all, it is *not* something that should be viewed as a separate or extra activity. Instead, it should be considered a practice and skill that can mutually reinforce and benefit other learning activities.

Lay the Groundwork

As educators, we have many opportunities to strengthen connections and work with young people to make meaning of the world together. We have the chance to support young people to tell their best stories, the kind that portray who they are, how they experience the world, and ultimately how they bring humanity to scholarship. To get started, consider the following suggestions:

- **Identify goals.** Students need to know why they are telling or listening to stories before they can proceed. Connecting storytelling to specific learning goals (such as community building, describing details, being persuasive, etc.) will also ensure stories integrate with learning.
- **Reinforce a storyteller's mindset.** Discuss what it means to be a storyteller. Being a storyteller means committing to affirming yourself, listening for connection, letting go of perfection, avoiding reading scripted stories word for word, and being willing to be playful and a little uncomfortable.
- **Create rituals and routines.** Making storytelling part of a class ritual or routine will help students get into the habit of developing their "storytelling muscles." Use stories as part of warm-ups, discussions about the big ideas and themes of a unit, or reflecting on new learning.
- **Use simple structures.** Ground students in a go-to structure to help them feel prepared. Sharing three-part structures or "story

arcs" can help them organize stories. An example is "Main Idea, Memory, Moral"—beginning with a main idea, then sharing a memory, and concluding with a takeaway lesson

- **Use prompts.** Prompts provide focus for a story, and it helps to offer two or three choices for story topics. More than three will lead students to spend too much time on their decision, and one choice is too limiting. Prompts can be as simple as providing three individual words and asking learners to tell a story inspired by one of those words. Sentence frames such as "Tell us about a time when . . ." can help learners invite their peers to tell stories—for instance, "Tell me about a time when you felt proud, you were helpful, you were angry, you had fun, you felt challenged."

- **Model connection.** Be genuinely interested in the stories students are sharing and demonstrate that interest with nonverbal behavior. After students tell their stories, share what resonated with you and what you remember most. Ask peers to answer similar questions, including what they learned about a person or what they are curious about.

Acknowledge the Emotional Nature of Storytelling

Although storytelling can be fun, it is also inherently emotional. Some young people are comfortable tapping into emotions, sharing them, or risking vulnerability. Some will feel more protective, especially if they have experienced traumas that make their stories likely to trigger negative emotions. We can't pretend young people are not whole, emotional beings. What happens outside school will inherently affect their lives in school.

Storytelling must be facilitated in a way that gives young people an entry to exploring and expressing emotions while giving them choice over how, when, and with whom they do that. When storytelling is part of a routine or ritual, they will be able to slowly open up, depending on their comfort level. To get started, begin with lighter topics so they can connect to emotions such as joy, happiness, accomplishment, or pride before using prompts that relate to more charged emotions. The goal is for them to feel more connected to their emotions and feel valued.

Set the Conditions for Storytelling

When setting the conditions for storytelling, begin by discussing why stories are important. Discussions about the value of stories offer young people a chance to reflect on why they should care about learning from others' stories and sharing personal experiences.

Norms are especially important in setting the stage for storytelling, for both speakers and listeners. Being clear about the length of each story and asking learners to time themselves can make them aware of how long they typically speak. Clear agreements are necessary to clarify who speaks when, as well as communicating to learners about which aspects of story-telling are "fixed" (e.g., following a structure) and which are "flexible" (e.g., topic choice).

Preparation time is an essential part of gaining the courage to share a story. Encourage learners to write stories as bulleted "talking points," or provide a graphic organizer with sentence starters (especially for the beginning and ending lines). To accommodate learners who do not feel ready to share, set a norm that allows for opening their story with the line "This is what I have so far."

To help young people get into "story mode," consider moving the classroom furniture, or sitting or standing in a circle to differentiate the experience from more typical academic learning. Establishing story-telling rituals also offers opportunities to recheck and reinforce the strong, identity-safe classroom culture discussed in Chapter 2.

Teaching Learners How to Listen

Just like telling stories, listening to them is an important skill that needs to be developed with support and practice. Listening enables the real-time development of relationships as young people and their teacher witness one another, seeing each other in new ways as a result of sharing stories. Listeners need clear instructions about what to do while peers tell their stories, including what to listen for and when and how to share reactions. Providing opportunities to practice the skill with a specific task will build everyone's ability to listen for connection.

At the elementary level, for instance, we worked with a 1st grade teacher who created listening cards for listeners to silently hold up as they identified key elements in a speaker's story. These included cards with both words and pictures saying "Who," "Where," "Details," and "Feelings." Beyond identifying elements, 1st graders were also able to give feedback in final reflections, saying "I liked how he included his feelings about his story" or "I wanted to know where her story was."

At the middle school level, it is helpful to practice note-taking skills during storytelling by using graphic organizers or note-catchers for listeners to capture what they hear. Beyond recording key phrases or ideas, graphic organizers can also provide listeners a chance to document their thoughts on how the storyteller delivered the story (e.g., gestures used, changes in tone, use of facial expressions).

High school students can take their listening skills to the next level by practicing their ability to recall and summarize what they have heard, using sentence starters such as "The main idea of the story was . . . ," "A detail that stood out to me was . . . ," "Something I noticed about the way the story was told was . . . ," "When you said this phrase, it made me think of . . . ."

Mining Memories for Stories

Chianne "Cloudy" Rhodes Carrier, a Sacramento-based poet and student, believes that all young people have stories in abundance. Her advice to young people is this: "You have years of stories inside of you that you want to tell, that you need to tell, that will help you if you tell them." Before anything can happen on paper, however, learners need opportunities to engage in oral communication to help them shape their ideas, listen to others, and practice speaking in detail.

No matter our age, we all have memories that make us feel things like pride, fear, embarrassment, excitement, and joy. According to Capital Storytelling, a Sacramento-based nonprofit focused on teaching the art of oral storytelling, our memories are the basis for the best and most authentic personal stories. In their *Oral Storytelling Workbook* (LeBron, 2021), they recommend the following protocol:

1. Set a timer for 2 minutes and ask students to write down as many memories as they can. Note: they don't have to write every detail of the memory down, just 1–2 words that can remind them or represent that memory is sufficient.

2. Ask students to look at their list. Let them know that all of these memories are a potential story! From that list, invite students to pick 3 memories that stand out to them and they would want to develop into a shareable story. Then narrow those top 3 down to 1 memory for their story.

3. Invite students to create their story by telling it or writing it down the way they remember it. Answering simple questions can provide a simple structure for them to follow, such as: What happened? How did it start? What happened next? And how did it end?

4. Share the stories as they are, as works in progress. They don't have to be perfect. Encourage them to start with the phrase, "This is what I have so far."

5. Invite students to reflect out loud about what they liked about their story, why they think they remembered it, and how the story impacted them. (pp. 4–7)

This protocol supports brainstorming to help young people get unstuck when they are working to communicate about specific themes. For example, have learners make a list of all the things they like to do in their free time. Then, have them choose one item from their list and tell a story about the first time they did that activity. This approach helps them narrow in on specific, meaningful moments that can be hard to recall when first prompted.

Using Storytelling to Support English Language Learners

Anyone can be a storyteller. For English language learners, the low-stakes nature of storytelling and its relationship to deep cultures of oral tradition make it an accessible entry point to connect with peers, especially around their personal journeys. English language development focuses heavily on speaking and listening to reach fluency, and proficiency assessments ask English language learners to answer questions about sequencing in stories, along with identifying key details and overall takeaways. Stories can also play a role in practicing conversation skills. The Stanford Center of Professional Development (2019), which supports educators in creating classroom cultures that enable constructive conversations, states:

> The bedrock principle of constructive conversation is that peer-to-peer discussions are incredibly valuable for students to develop critical communication and language skills, while also providing plenty of leeway for them to work out new ideas, make mistakes and think more critically about the subject matter. Unlike traditional teaching methods, which center on rote memorization and repetition, constructive conversation builds knowledge and language proficiency by promoting interactions between students that allow for spontaneous, critical thinking. (para. 10)

Elementary schools already place significant emphasis on the narrative genre when students are reading and writing. Integrating speaking and listening skills into this process is critical for all students (including English language learners). Velia Casillas, a 4th grade teacher in Los Angeles, believes storytelling is an important tool for supporting English language learners, who have rich cultural experiences. Stories shared in the classroom allow them to explain those experiences in vivid detail. She states, "For second-language learners, providing them a safe space for storytelling sets a strong foundation on which to build all of the other skills and strategies that they have to master to become fluent in English." Ms. Casillas regularly uses storytelling as a strategy to support the English language learners in her class to deepen their connection with their classmates while tapping into their existing cultural funds of knowledge. She continues:

> [Storytelling] helps them exercise the amount of details because when they storytell, their classmates are naturally curious. So they want to know more, which helps them because then when they put pencil to paper they are not just going to say, "I liked my birthday party. It was fun." They are going to be like, "I had a pinata, and we had a DJ and we made birria." They are going to tell all those details. If you just give them a prompt and go straight to the writing, it wouldn't work.

Addressing Learners' Resistance

Your learners may include some who, despite your efforts, will still feel that they have no stories to tell or that their stories don't matter. When you introduce storytelling, you may be met with comments such as "I don't have any stories" (maybe accompanied by rolling eyes or crossed arms). When encountering resistance, it is important to remember that all learners start from different places. Some young people may take very well to the invitation to respond to a prompt and start talking, whereas others may need some structure to support their thinking.

Using Games

One effective way to address resistance or reluctance is to ask learners to share their interests and preferences before diving into a story. Two useful games to get things going are Hot Seat and This or That.

To play Hot Seat, begin by picking one student to sit in the "hot seat," and set a timer for two minutes. Ask the class to ask the student a random question. The goal of the student in the hot seat is to answer as many random questions as possible in the two minutes. Students in the hot seat can choose to say "pass" if they can't come up with a response or if they don't feel comfortable answering. You can model this for your students first, as they are likely already comfortable asking you questions. This activity is useful because it gets students accustomed to standing in front of their peers (one of the major barriers to public speaking is just being able to say anything in front of a large group of people), and they are only sharing things about their preferences and interests, not yet telling a full story.

To play This or That, begin by listing a comparison (or a series of comparisons) on the board, such as hot or cold, dogs or cats, music or books, breakfast or dinner. Students then pick which thing they prefer and share out loud one or two reasons why. This activity can be done in pairs, small groups, or as a whole class. Encourage students to elaborate if they say things such as "I just like . . ." or "I just do," reminding them that the goal is to get to know the *why* of their choice. This activity works because there is usually a moment or experience that informs their preference, and recalling that moment or experience is where stories begin.

Remind young people that meaningful stories start small. What makes a story meaningful is what it helps someone remember about the person telling it and the topic they discussed. Aspects of self can unconsciously reveal themselves in the act of sharing something about ourselves or even listening to a story as a group.

Tapping into Joy and Laughter

Stories don't have to begin with a big meaty prompt to be meaningful. In fact, as noted, getting to meaningful and authentic stories can start with something small. That something might be a color and an accessible feeling, such as joy. This simple, two-part exercise that starts with an object and a color can inspire students to tell joyful stories:

1. Put students into groups of two or three and assign each group a color. Give the groups 5 to 10 minutes to list as many items as they can that bring them joy and correspond to the color they were assigned—for example, things that are blue that bring them joy. Ask the groups to then share their list and some reasons why each item brings them joy.
2. Ask students to pick one item from a different color's list to serve as their inspiration for a quick, on-the-spot, true personal story.

Students should start their story with "Speaking of . . . ." After each story is shared, invite listeners to tell what they remember from each speaker's story.

Sometimes it can be helpful to find models of storytellers in non-traditional places, such as comedy. Stories that are rooted in joy and laughter are often the most impactful and memorable. A poet and stand-up comedian we interviewed recommends a format to infuse jokes and poems with storytelling. He explains:

> The storytelling format that works for comedy and poetry is: start with a premise. What's the idea? Then add the setting. Then you have to play on emotions, whether the audience's emotion or your emotion. Then [add] the dilemma from the setting and the emotion. A conflict or a plot twist, then the climax. And once I put all that together I write down what I can and mind-map my stories better.

Invite young people to model their stories in a similar format, rooting them in comedy as an accessible entry point to connect to the magic of storytelling before diving into deeper emotions. What we find humorous as people also speaks to aspects of our culture and identity. Plus, laughing together is a great way to build community!

Promoting Bonds and Friendships

Writer Patty Digh (n.d.) said it best: "The shortest distance between two people is one story." Classrooms need to be places where young people can build and strengthen community and express the full range of who they are today and who they want to be in the future. Community cannot be built in a space where individuals within it cannot or do not express the full range of their humanity.

Young people are constantly trying to make sense of the public and private aspects of their identity. Every day they are having an internal dialogue as they try to answer the question *Who am I?* How much or how little of that dialogue they share out loud is determined by how welcome they feel in the spaces they live and learn in and how many opportunities they have to speak.

Much of who they are, how they identify themselves, and even their confidence is determined by peer connections. A 2008 study (Bauminger et al.) published in the *Journal of Social and Personal Relationships*, entitled "Intimacy in Adolescent Friendship: The Roles of Attachment, Coherence, and Self-Disclosure," found that adolescents need to initiate bonds with their friends and to feel like the world makes sense (coherence). The researchers also found that the way they build those intimate bonds is by self-disclosing (sharing feelings and stories about themselves). Telling stories is a great way to help young people build bonds with one another as they make sense of the world together. When they tell a story, they create some kind of meaning or narrative that helps them share aspects of who they are and how they see the world, both critical elements in shaping their identity.

Qualities of "Good" Storytelling

How do we assess and grade storytelling? Because stories are personal and vulnerable in nature, they are harder to grade and evaluate critically. If storytelling is introduced as an ungraded, low-stakes activity, learners may not feel sufficiently motivated or invested. To account for the unique nature of storytelling, evaluation criteria must encourage and guide storytellers to communicate their humanity. Such criteria include the following:

- **Risk taking and effort.** Is the student stretching themselves? Was it evident that the student prepared, practiced, or incorporated feedback they received? Did they commit to their performance?
- **Delivery and intentionality.** Did the student make clear and apparent choices in the way they delivered their story? Were there distinct emotions and tones? Did they vary volume or speed?
- **Delivery effectiveness.** Did the student make delivery choices that were convincing or believable? Were you drawn in by the story

or overall performance? Were you swayed or surprised by the message? Was the story focused?

- **Authenticity.** Were you able to get a sense of the student as a person and their beliefs, background, identity, concerns, opinions, or ideas?

Good storytelling uses powerful language, creative sequencing of ideas, compelling messages, and clear structure with just enough detail and context to clarify but not bog down the narrative. Clarity is especially important. To help a listener follow the story, it must be clear about the main character, the central theme or problem, and a sequence of events. Clarity can also come in the choices about length (how long it takes to tell the story), purpose (why the story is being told), direction (the specific way the speaker decides to take the prompt), and adaptability (how the story is told and modified depending on where it is shared and who it is shared with).

Powerful stories introduce vulnerability, either through the emotional content that is revealed or through the fact that the speaker is putting themselves out there to speak at all. The speaker has a choice in how they want to display that vulnerability. Stories should make the listener feel something, which is a core part of why stories foster connections. What are the visceral reactions listeners have when witnessing a story? Maybe they breathe differently during certain moments or get chills at a speaker's word choice. These reactions are feelings emerging as a result of the story being told.

Validity is also an important consideration—that is, the content of a story should validate or shed light on a relatable experience. The act of relating a story and being heard helps the storyteller feel validated and encouraged to take up space.

To make storytelling more rigorous, consider choosing prompts that encourage deep thinking, increasing or decreasing the amount of time for the story, and giving the audience specific things to listen for. Repetition also encourages learners to engage in "oral editing" as they practice telling their story, incorporate feedback from peers, and then retell their story to make it more effective.

Reflection and Feedback

Reflection and feedback are important accompaniments to storytelling. From the standpoint of social and emotional learning, reflection enables young people to build self-awareness and community connection. Learners are constantly negotiating which aspects of their identity they can share with others and which ones they must keep private in order to blend in, belong, or survive. Because of this, it is important to make space for students to reflect on their own, with one another, out loud, or in writing after telling their stories. Here are some reflection questions or sentence starters you can use after stories are shared:

- The next time I tell a story about [topic] I will say more about . . . .
- What is something our stories about [topic] have in common?
- How did you feel before, during, and after telling your story?
- What is something you would have said if you had more time?
- What is something you learned about yourself/your peers after hearing these stories?

When giving feedback to young people on stories, strike a balance between affirmations and adjustments related to both the content and delivery. Here are some ways to do that:

- **Be specific about what stood out.** Name the specific moments or word choices in the story that stood out, what resonated, and what you learned about the student as a result. For example, "When you talked about your grandparents throwing you a birthday party, I could tell you were grateful and that you really love them. They must really mean a lot to you."
- **Ask for more details from a place of curiosity.** Naming the places in a story that left you wondering, confused, or wanting more detail is a helpful way to improve the student's organization and delivery skills over time. For example, "I liked how you talked about going to the store to buy a new bike. You mentioned you tried riding

different bikes before you chose one. I wanted to hear more about the other bikes you didn't like so I could understand what made the bike you chose so special." Rooting feedback in what you were wondering is a useful way to help students improve parts in a story where they could have gone into more detail.

- **Give challenges.** As students build their comfort level with telling stories, styles may naturally emerge. Take note of these and use them as a way to push students' skills by naming a strength they have and then giving them a challenge for their next story. For example, "You are great at sharing your inner thoughts in your stories! In your next story, I'd like to see you share more about how the other people in your stories are feeling, what they are saying or doing with you, so there is more balance."
- **Help learners give one another feedback.** Once again, sentence starters can support a balance between affirmation and adjustment. These can include "One thing I liked about your story was . . . ," "A detail that stood out in your story was . . . ," and "One way to improve your story would be . . . ."

Final Takeaways

Storytelling is rewarding when it intentionally connects to youth voice. The classroom is a critical container where learning, discovery, and self-mastery take place. Sharing stories within this container is an act that is equal parts empowering, transformative, and revolutionary. A special kind of magic happens when we are able to use our voice to speak our truth, shed light on injustices, and advocate for ourselves or our community. There is also something inherently joyful, powerful, and liberating in the act of telling true personal stories about ourselves, our experiences, and our worldviews.

Telling our stories helps us own and take pride in our identities, share our convictions and opinions with the world, and witness our peers as they find their power. Making space for stories in the classroom can help us disrupt moments when young people feel invisible. Teaching them how to tell stories and offering them a brave space to do so is the best way to address their need for acceptance. Ultimately, the goal of bringing storytelling into your classroom should be to create a low-stakes, high-value way to deepen connections, celebrate similarities and differences, and share in the critical (and often missing) "humanity time" that many of us need to feel whole and seen, and to heal together, one story at a time.

5

Debate to Encourage Equitable Participation

In a divided society, debate may seem like the last strategy an educator would want to employ in the classroom. Many educators and young people alike envision the shouting matches often seen on political stages and fear having to speak about unfamiliar issues or feeling out of control. Too often, debate is reserved for those perceived as the "good kids" and the already confident speakers.

In fact, the structure and facilitation of debate make it safer than some other forms of communication for young people to engage in, because the rules encourage people to listen to different views. Bob Litan (2020) of the Brookings Institution defines *debate* as "structured, civil discussion" that involves at least two sides to an issue, focuses on substance, features time limits for each side, and compels speakers to persuade an audience about how to make informed choices, incorporate new information, and identify ways to reach consensus. He continues, "[T]he ability to discuss formally, but in a civil way, multiple sides of any topic is a skill that can be learned and, once learned, confers substantial benefits to individuals and society" (p. 87). He quotes commentator Van Jones: "Debate is the lifeblood of democracy, after all. Disagreement is a good thing—even heated disagreement. Only in a dictatorship does everyone have to agree" (pp. 87–88).

Debate as an Educational Tool

Given Litan's definition, it comes as no surprise that debate is one of the most comprehensive speaking formats for addressing standards across all grade levels. As early as 1st grade, learners are expected to respond to and build on comments from others, developing their skills to eventually become 12th graders who are expected by academic standards to "respond thoughtfully to diverse perspectives, synthesize comments, claims, and evidence made on all sides of an issue, resolve contradictions, and determine what information is required to deepen investigation" (National Governors Association Center for Best Practices & Council of Chief State School Officers, 2010). The ability to engage in healthy debate is valuable to preparing for future careers (particularly those that are innovative and entrepreneurial), securing jobs, challenging fake news, and encouraging civic engagement and interest in social issues (Litan, 2020). In addition, careful and deliberate listening is one of the most important capabilities taught through debate because it is impossible to participate in a debate without structured note taking and the ability to simultaneously listen and synthesize. These benefits are the product of debates that are geared toward fostering understanding through clear facilitation and should be viewed as a protocol for conversations about contrast and courage. Classroom debates do not, and should not, look like present-day debates by candidates seeking public office.

When facilitated equitably, debate can give young people the confidence and skill needed to navigate places of power in the future. When girls and young people of color feel confident that they know how to speak and participate, it becomes easier to quiet any internalized beliefs that their voice is somehow "less than" or the nerves that accompany high-stakes situations involving people in power. According to debate educators Melissa Graham and Les Lynn, English language learners particularly benefit from debate skills to advocate for their needs and their families as well as to counteract the very real fear of humiliation in front of their peers. By requiring debaters to research and debate both sides of an issue, they are less likely to view others as "the enemy" and more likely to remain open-minded, learning to ask questions before judgment and to explain their points so that everyone can understand them (Litan, 2020).

Our world is burdened with deep-seated institutional, interpersonal, and internalized oppression. In such an environment, preparing young people to understand diverse viewpoints, develop empathy, and navigate inequities in service of a healthier democracy is worth the work.

There are many benefits of debating:

- Promotes taking a perspective and understanding diverse viewpoints
- Encourages empathy and open-mindedness
- Develops confidence
- Promotes organization and structure in thinking, writing, and speaking
- Provides practice in persuasive and argumentative writing
- Furthers literacy skills
- Expands academic language
- Enables challenging fake news
- Builds research skills
- Improves ability to explain concepts clearly
- Refines questioning skills
- Fosters careful and deliberate listening
- Develops note-taking skills
- Enables adapting to different audiences
- Contributes to career and leadership preparation
- Improves collaboration and teamwork skills
- Enhances ability to interview for and secure jobs
- Encourages civic engagement
- Develops interest in and understanding of social issues
- Promotes advocacy and self-advocacy skills
- Supports participation in a healthier democracy

Equity Through Debate

When done well, debate can be a powerful tool to address equity and promote a classroom environment that is inclusive and healing. We've already noted its positive effects for girls, young people of color, and

English language learners, in particular. With a structured protocol that includes clear guidelines for engagement, debate makes the "rules of the game" visible, enabling everyone to know what to expect from social interactions that are often hidden and implicit.

Structure can bring a sense of safety and protection for those who struggle socially. For people on the autism spectrum, for instance, knowing the flow and order of a conversation, as well as where and how they can participate, takes the guesswork out of an already stressful process of navigating complex social situations. The back-and-forth protocol structure itself can counteract the tendency for one group to interrupt another (e.g., for men to interrupt women), and the templated approach for prepared speeches makes the conversation more accessible when English is not the debater's first language. Having a predictable routine brings a sense of safety and comfort when discussing challenging and controversial issues, and debate topics can help clarify the central issue being discussed.

The project-based learning organization PBLWorks identifies *knowledge of students, cognitive demand, literacy,* and *shared power* as "four equity levers" in helping every young person develop, participate, and persist through challenging tasks (Field, 2021). Here we make the connection between debate and these equity levers, and illustrate how debate can be used to address them:

- **Knowledge of students.** Helping young people express their opinions and even craft their own debate topics makes it easier for educators to understand more about who young people are as individuals, which can be a challenge in large classes. Over time, debate topics also offer the opportunity for all learners (even the educators) to learn more about their own perspectives, cultural lenses, and biases, which is important for improving practice and strengthening relationships.
- **Cognitive demand.** The process of debate is in itself cognitively demanding, and clear structures and practice over time can help young people engage in complex intellectual work and surpass preconceived notions about their ability.

- **Literacy.** When implemented effectively, debate drives literacy development, as long as careful attention is paid to make sure debaters use evidence that includes culturally relevant texts and debate rounds include diverse viewpoints and language practices.
- **Shared power.** What debate does especially well is to promote shared power in the classroom, with young people leading conversations and teamwork, actively shaping the learning process, and supporting everyone's learning, even that of the teacher.

By activating these four levers, debate can be an equitable teaching practice that transforms classrooms into exciting places to challenge assumptions.

Debate and Intersectionality

Whereas storytelling is a more effective means for young people to discuss their personal identities, debate is an ideal way to acknowledge the layers of complexity behind a controversial issue. It prompts young people to better understand the history and context behind worldviews, question whether policies and actions marginalize people, and propose plans for how to address marginalization. Debate topics can directly consider how forms of oppression intersect and ask students to consider the impact of those intersections, which is at the heart of Kimberlé Crenshaw's work on intersectionality. Rather than resorting to personal attacks, young people are encouraged to take a macro look at controversial issues and movements, such as how women of color are portrayed in media or how social movements can best advance the rights of people at the intersection of race, gender, and disability.

When topics are especially sensitive, it certainly becomes a challenge to send both the message "Your perspective and experience are valid and should be heard" and the message "It is important to be able to understand and articulate how others view the world." In these cases, topics to avoid are ones in which harmful arguments cannot be avoided.

When Debate Is Inequitable

Like any other instructional approach, debate is not inherently equitable. Inequitable debate is characterized by some voices dominating others, people being interrupted, hurtful insults and attacks, personal emotions overwhelming the conversation, and yelling, with ideas getting lost in the chaos.

Avoiding controversial and challenging conversations in the classroom is also inequitable, however, because it prevents learners from directly engaging with different viewpoints (and teaching them how to navigate difference). A classroom where everyone always has to agree promotes an echo chamber and sends the message that you don't belong if you don't agree.

Getting Started

A consistent theme across the inequities just mentioned involves actions that make debate confusing, unbalanced, unfair, and without direction in an environment without respect. That said, educators and facilitators need as much practice as learners do. Debate is not something to avoid because of fear of making an error. Young people of all ages catch on quickly to debate structures, and although educators and facilitators may need to do a lot of upfront work, debate can eventually become a regularly used strategy that learners can lead and improve over time.

Schedule Debate to Advance Learning

Before exploring ways to structure debate and what to debate about, the first question to ask is "When is a debate the appropriate way to teach desired skills or content?" Although debate can be a great way to engage learners and increase class participation, it should be an integrated part of teaching the content, not an add-on activity. Debate should advance learning for each student and be used intentionally to advance equity. According to one of our debaters, 17-year-old Jacob Klein,

> Debate can tie into whatever else is being taught at the time. For example, if you are reading about a historical event or even reading a novel, there are so many things that can be debated. For example, character relationships in a novel or the impact of X historical event. This can

give the class a better understanding of what they are reading/learning. Also, debate can improve the quality of argumentative writing.

Across grade levels, we have found that debates work best at the start of units, as a tool to explore a theme or driving question that contextualizes the rest of the learning. As a best practice in project-based learning, debate can be used as an "entry event" (rather than as a culminating project, as is most typically done), to spark interest and fulfill the science of learning principle of "engagement first" (Schwartz & Bransford, 1998).

However, debate can also be useful as learning progresses. In the middle of units, it can be used in places where you may have typically held a discussion, as a way to deepen a subsequent discussion, or when you want the class to propose solutions to a dilemma. At the end of units, debates can be used to have young people apply their learning and research to address a deeper issue or question.

Use Debate Across Subject Areas

Debate works best when there is a controversial issue that needs to be resolved and there are clearly two sides that both warrant exploration. Most people probably think of debate as something easily incorporated into history, social studies, and government classes, where it can be used to have learners consider the impact of an event, question the morality or ethics behind political actions, or suggest plans and policies to solve enduring issues. But it can be incorporated into other content areas as well. In English, debate is best suited to conversations about broad themes or exploring the relevance of themes in literature, such as debating the topic "Girls today can see themselves reflected in modern beauty standards" when studying Toni Morrison's *The Bluest Eye*. Famous quotes or tweets can also be a useful trigger for a debate on whether that quote is true or not. It is often more challenging to integrate debate into a math lesson, but learners can benefit from a topic that asks them to reflect on their learning, such as "Fractions are too hard to understand," where one side argues about what they find challenging and the other side defends the concept and explains it. Using debate for learners' self-reflection can help you understand their progress and encourage them to teach others. In math, debate can also be used as a way for learners to discuss the best method for solving a problem and to explain their process and thinking, while also making personal connections to what they learn. In elective classes such as art and PE, debates on any topic can also be important team-building and leadership exercises, especially when young people facilitate the debates.

Develop Literacy Skills Across Grade Levels

Beyond its role in exploring content, debate should be used to develop literacy skills. If you are teaching a unit that requires young people to practice argumentation, explain and justify their claims, and practice note taking and collaboration, then debate is ideal for a range of ages. At The Practice Space, we work with children as young as 7, and we find that the clear rules of debate work well as long as the wording of the topic itself is accessible, connected to their lives, and somewhat familiar to them. Topics that ask young learners to suggest solutions or solve problems work particularly well. At the middle school level, debate requires more scaffolding to help preteens feel less self-conscious about taking a stand on issues, but they find moral and philosophical topics especially engaging because there is not a clear "right" or "wrong" answer. In high school, a mixture of straightforward and complex topics is useful to give everyone an entry point to participate.

Craft Debate Topics That Promote a Stance

To make debate inclusive and accessible, the most important decision you can make is the topic and its wording. Debate topics (otherwise known as "resolutions" or "motions") are always crafted as sentences that clearly promote a side, as opposed to questions that lend themselves better to discussions. In any subject, transforming a discussion question into a sentence prompt allows two sides to emerge: one that supports the sentence as written and one that offers an alternative. Aside from clearly articulating an issue, debate topics can be starting points for problem solving, reflection, and team building.

In general, debate topics fall into three categories:

- **Fact topics** are topics that ask young people to debate about whether something is true or not, such as "Video games are too violent." This type of topic is good for practicing argument construction and using concrete examples.
- **Value topics** ask young people to explore the morality, justice, or ethics behind an issue or to prioritize one thing over another, as in "The United States has a moral obligation to help developing countries" or "Teen privacy should be valued over parents' responsibility to protect their child." These kinds of topics work best when the goal is to have the class learn about philosophical principles or to discuss worldviews or hypothetical situations.
- **Policy topics** require young people to outline plans of action and, in most cases, use evidence to support their plan. Examples of topics that involve a clear actor and action include "The United States government should increase funding for education," "Financial literacy should become a graduation requirement," and "Private cars should be banned in large cities."

When crafting a topic, it is easiest to start with a topic area or general theme, such as technology, entertainment, safety, liberty, or crime. From there, ask yourself, *What is the core issue I want my class to explore?* For instance, for the topic area "safety," you may want learners to explore the issue of gun control. Creating the topic itself then involves creating a sentence that takes a clear and strong stance on that issue—for example, "Gun possession is justified when communities are unsafe." The wording of the topic should be an interpretation that is as respectful as possible of a particular side and that guides learners to think about different ways of solving problems. For instance, wording the gun topic to be about community safety leaves an opening for the opposite side to argue about different ways of addressing safety. To be inclusive of different beliefs, worldviews, and experiences, topics about particularly divisive issues should ask learners how to address a problem or what they would propose to be the most inclusive and effective solution to a problem.

It is often tempting to create topics that have examples embedded in them, such as "The recent examples of Asian hate crimes justify people carrying guns to defend themselves." Mentioning examples in topics prevents young people from researching the issue as a whole and then bringing in the example themselves and justifying why they think that example is relevant. The more clash that the topic inspires the better, as long as the topic is still "debatable" (Heinrichs, 2007).

Litan (2020) suggests topics that are not well-suited for debates are ones that contest well-established laws of physics or mathematics, the existence of events that have been thoroughly documented by historians and archeologists, and subjects where one side would have to defend beliefs that are fundamentally inconsistent with basic principles and beliefs. Such topics may be better suited to direct instruction. It is challenging to decide what should be off limits, but the ultimate decision depends on comfort level (while also not avoiding issues purely out of fear), knowing your students, and making sure the debate will result in a productive exploration of an issue and avoid harmful arguments.

Advice from our debaters emphasizes the level of difficulty and relevance of a topic. For example, 15-year-old Mercy Niyi-Awolesi suggests, "When selecting a topic, try not to choose something too complicated or too simple. It keeps students interested." Fifteen-year-old Vidita Bhatt encourages teachers to

> Start off with topics students are passionate about, but make sure to explore various stances in areas they may not be familiar with. Having to argue positions that you've never considered forces students to analyze from different perspectives and broadens their views and how they approach things they might disagree with.

Seventeen-year-old Jacob Klein concurs:

> I would suggest starting with smaller topics like dogs vs. cats or when to put milk in cereal. Students may already have an opinion on those topics. If that is the case, challenge them by putting them on the opposite side of what they think (at least during some debates), so they can get a deeper understanding.

This advice from young people highlights the importance of including easy topics to capture their energy and attention but also ramping up the difficulty to push their thinking. Challenging topics can be even more engaging than simple ones (e.g., dogs versus cats) because their complexity pushes debaters to think about real issues they may not have encountered.

For more guidance on creating topics and designing debates, see Resource 4 and Resource 7 (www.practice-space.org/debate-guide/) in The Practice Space's *Debate Guide* (Baines, 2020d).

Differentiate for Different Learners

As you come up with debate topics, it is important to differentiate for different learners. To support literacy, express topics with words that all students can understand (or that you will define and explain before the debate begins). Balance productive struggle with enough familiarity to ensure equitable engagement and validation of learners' funds of knowledge. Support English language learners by offering a digital glossary of key definitions that they can translate using digital tools, and a starter kit of research links to gain more general information, history, and context about a topic (without doing all the research for them).

Involving young people and their families in coming up with topics can also increase a debate's relevance to their lives. We often have young people and families suggest topic areas first, before we refine the exact wording, or we propose three topic options and have them select their topic to encourage student choice and give them the opportunity to select one that is accessible.

Most important, debates must be equitable, ethical, and sensitive to the experiences of young people. Remember that for some, an issue may be deeply real and not just the topic for an exercise. The assignment of debaters to one or the other side of a debate has important implications. For example, it is not appropriate to ask someone who has a relative in the criminal justice system to defend the death penalty. Similarly, asking a person of color to defend racist viewpoints or a victim of sexual assault to defend abusers is unethical and counterproductive to education. When oppression is part of everyday lived experience, it is not something to be debated; instead, storytelling or self-advocacy presentations are more meaningful and equitable approaches.

Ensuring Equitable Debate Structures

The clear structure of debate can advance equity by helping young people feel more comfortable, safe, and protected, because they know what to expect. Every debate can be boiled down to the following structure: prework, preparation time, opening speeches, responses and cross-examination, closing speeches, and reflection and feedback.

Prework

Prework begins well before the actual event. It is the untimed process of learning how to debate, including learning the protocol, understanding how to construct an argument and write speeches, and practicing how to ask questions. Vocabulary lists for English language learners are helpful at this stage, in addition to having them listen to podcasts or videos in their native language. Prework is when the direct instruction happens and when warm-ups and drills give learners opportunities to practice and gradually ease into debate.

For more experienced debaters, prework can also involve becoming more familiar with current events and world issues and setting up routines and habits that will serve them in a debate. Debaters should build habits such as listening to news podcasts, reading news headlines each day, or picking an area of focus (e.g., the economy, crime, health, education) and learning key terms and information about notable people or events.

Preparation Time

Preparation time, or prep time, refers to the timed period after an actual debate topic is announced. The amount of prep time varies widely across debate protocols, ranging from as little as five minutes to as long as several months or even a year. During prep time, debaters work individually, in pairs, or in small groups on an assigned side to a specific topic. They learn to manage their time effectively by spending time on brainstorming, clarifying background information and key terms, sketching opening speeches, deciding on roles, and anticipating what the other side might say. Debaters discover quickly that they need a clear approach for their preparation time, which develops higher-order strategic thinking skills, strong collaboration, organization, and time management. Before and after their first debate, it is useful for them to reflect on best practices for prep time and share strategies for how to better prepare for their next debates. Best practices for prep time can be presented as a checklist, including time for the following:

- Conducting overview research on the main issue to figure out why it is being debated and collecting any useful examples
- Brainstorming as many points as possible and outlining them into an opening speech
- Deciding who will say what (if the structure involves teams or partners)
- Anticipating what the other side might say, and how to respond
- Practicing oral delivery

Although these practices can seem too complex for elementary grades, these kinds of checklists are familiar to younger children as rules to help organize their preparation. Rewording these best practices as questions and directive steps can help make them more accessible, as in the following examples:

- Discuss with your partner: Why is this topic important?
- Make a list: What are four to six reasons why our side of the debate is correct?
- Look it up: What are two to three examples to support our side?
- Put it in the worksheet: Which argument should we say first, next, and last?
- Divide it up: Who will say which argument?

- Practice time: Have we tried running through our speech at least two times?

One of the most important pieces of advice you can give debaters is this: *Do not write down everything in full sentences.* Point out that note writing for oral communication is different from regular writing, because debaters just need something that they can refer to and understand as they present out loud. This realization can be particularly freeing for students with learning disabilities and for English language learners, because they can participate without fearing that people will judge their spelling or written-sentence construction. Outlines, bullet points, and abbreviations are a key part of preparing quickly and efficiently, and these skills are useful in life beyond the classroom.

Opening Speeches

The opening speech typically contains the following parts: (1) statement of the topic and the side being debated, (2) definition of key terms, (3) two to four different "contentions" or structured arguments, and (4) a concluding statement and urge to vote for their side. *Contentions* are the most important content to teach to beginning debaters before participating in a debate. When instructing learners on how to structure an argument, teach them to label their contentions by saying "My first contention is ...," "My second contention is ...," and so on.

A contention is made up of the following elements:

- **Claims** consist of a single, concise sentence that describes a specific opinion, such as "Plastic packaging should be banned because it harms the environment." Although the debate topic itself is a claim, debaters articulate more specific claims in their contentions.
- **Warrants** are personal and historical examples, evidence and research, and logical reasoning that support the claim and explain it in more depth.
- **Impacts** are the significance or implications of the claim, such as the benefits or harms that result, or why the claim matters to the debate.

An argument must have all three elements to be considered valid. The argument structure relates to that in other content disciplines such as the scientific or textual claims, evidence, and reasoning covered in English language arts or science. The difference in debate is that it is important for debaters to explicitly state why their argument matters. In contrast to textual or scientific argumentation, stories and narrative examples are encouraged alongside facts and evidence. Templates like the one in Figure 5.1 not only are helpful for English language learners and students with learning disabilities, but also serve as a universal guide to help young people structure their ideas.

Responses and Cross-Examination

After the opening speech, the next few speeches in a debate include time for debaters to respond to one another or ask questions, or both. For responses, it is good practice to help debaters learn sentence starters to

---

FIGURE 5.1
Template for Opening Speeches

1. Statement of the topic and the side being debated:
   — "Today, we will be talking about . . . ."
   — "We will argue in favor of . . ." or "We will argue against . . . ."
2. Definition of key terms:
   — "For clarity, by [key term from resolution], we mean [dictionary definition, or debater's definition of term]."
3. Contentions (including claims, warrants, and impacts):
   — "Our first contention is . . . . This is because . . . . This is important because . . . . (If multiple debaters are giving the speech together, then one speaker will say, "Now on to my partner's contention.")
   — "Our second contention is . . . . This is because . . . . This is important because . . . . (If multiple debaters are giving the speech together, then one speaker will say, "Now on to my partner's contention.")
   — "Our third contention is . . . . This is because . . . . This is important because . . . ."
4. Concluding statement and urge to vote for their side:
   — "In conclusion, . . ."
   — "For all these reasons, you should vote for our team."

be able to respond to each argument in an organized manner. A common technique is called "four-step refutation." It goes like this:

1. **"My opponent claims** . . . ." (Summarize or quote the specific argument the student is responding to.)
2. **"But I disagree** . . . ." (It is not necessary to disagree with every argument. Instead, debaters should be selective about when they do want to disagree and use phrasing such as "But I disagree, because the argument is irrelevant/does not support the thesis/ undermines the thesis/is outweighed by stronger arguments to the contrary." It is critical that the responding student be as clear about his own claim as he is about the claim he is responding to.)
3. **"Because** . . . ." (Provide clear and logical reasons for the claim being made.)
4. **"And therefore** . . . ." (Explain why this argument matters in the debate.)

In debate, the technique of clearly identifying the claim and/or the number of the argument the debater is responding to, as well as the argument the debater is making (in particular, numbering multiple arguments in a clear and organized way), is known as *signposting*. Here's an example: "In their second contention, they say . . . . Instead, we argue . . . ." Highlighting the need for organization helps the debate remain systematic and easy to follow, and it avoids mixing arguments together or having the debate devolve into a shouting match.

Debates can also include time for cross-examination, a period of questioning that can help clarify key terms, ask about elements that were missed or confusing, or push the opponent to justify claims and provide more evidence and examples. Debaters sometimes struggle to ask questions, so it is a good idea to post question sentence starters in the classroom or have a minilesson to practice crafting *how, why,* and *what* questions to either clarify areas of confusion or ask the other team to elaborate further or explore hypothetical situations. For a student who is struggling to come up with a question, the simplest option is "Please explain [X argument that the questioner did not follow]" or "Can you give an example of [one of their arguments]?"

Closing Speeches

In closing speeches, debaters should not bring up new arguments; instead they should focus on telling the story of the debate round, synthesizing key issues, and weighing areas of disagreement. To help debaters synthesize their points, it can be helpful to post sample phrases such as "What this round comes down to is . . ." or "The heart of this issue is . . ." or "In their world, they have . . . and in our world, we have . . . ." Sentence starters for closing speeches, like the ones shown in Figure 5.2, can be helpful for new debaters and English language learners because of the emphasis on summarizing the arguments that have been made. It can be easier for beginners either to give the opening or closing speeches (rather than have to speak spontaneously) or to share a speech with another person and focus on saying one thing.

Reflection and Feedback

Once the debate has finished, reflection and feedback are an important part of ensuring that the debate has resulted in significant learning. Providing listeners, outside judges, and audience members with a rubric, a guided ballot sheet, or even a simple checklist goes a long way to helping

---

FIGURE 5.2
Sentence Starters for Closing Speeches

- "In today's debate, we've been arguing about . . . ."
- "The first reason to vote for our team is . . . ." (Reasons must include claims, warrants, and impacts.)
- "The second reason to vote for our team is . . . ."
- "In their world, they have . . . ."
- "Our world leads to . . . ."
- "For all these reasons, you should vote for our team."

people avoid their own biases and judge the debate based simply on the arguments presented.

Although debaters always want to know who won the debate, we recommend having a few practice debates with no winner or loser so that they get used to receiving feedback and writing down areas where they want to improve. Feedback should be specific and actionable, pointing out which arguments were most compelling and which needed more explanation and support. Although comments on delivery are important, they should not be the overwhelming focus for class or teacher commentary. Comments such as "I like that you were passionate" or "You said too many 'ums'" are too vague and not suitable for an in-depth activity that requires immense effort. Feedback that identifies specific actions ("Pause between main arguments") is more helpful than vague feedback ("Make your speech easier to follow"), and identifying positive actions ("Maintain eye contact until your last word") is often more effective than telling debaters what not to do ("Don't trail off at the end of the speech"). Debate is a challenging activity that requires a great deal of effort from speakers, so audience feedback should respect their hard work through thoughtful, specific, and helpful comments.

After a few practice sessions, it is helpful to have a debate with winners and losers. Doing so drives improvement and helps young people process failure, so long as there are many opportunities to try again in the future. It is critical, however, to emphasize that the losing debaters could have won the round with a different strategy. Laying the strategy out for them can be empowering, especially when compared with the alternative message that the other debaters were "better." Also, pointing out their strengths can help them feel that a win next time is within reach. Timing matters when introducing the element of competition. There should not be winners and losers if young people do not yet understand how to do a debate or if they are still working on the goal of participating.

Tips for Structuring Debate

Determining which structure of debate will work best involves a few key decisions. Here are questions to ask yourself:

1. **How big will the debate groups be?** This decision often depends on how much time you want to spend on debate. Debates can be one-on-one, two-on-two, three-on-three, or even half the class versus the other half. The decision about grouping also involves figuring out whether you want learners to jointly present each speech or whether you want them to figure out who will deliver each speech.

2. **How much preparation time will be required and provided?** Some forms of debate give debaters months to prepare and others give them 10 to 20 minutes. This decision is largely driven by how often you want learners to be able to practice their skills and how much research you want them to do.

3. **How much time will be allotted for each speech?** This decision will be based on how long you want the total debate to be, how many arguments you want the debaters to make, and how deeply you want them to go into the topic.

Debate Formats

Because debate is so cognitively demanding, it requires protocols to scaffold the experience and make it more inclusive. Competitive high school debate uses multiple forms, including Parliamentary Debate, Policy Debate, Lincoln-Douglas Debate, Public Forum, Student Congress, Big Questions Debate, and World Schools Debate. Although these formats may be too long and technical to use in the classroom, knowing their names can be helpful when searching for video examples, prewritten topics, or reference articles. Outside of competitive speech and debate, other out-of-school organizations use simulation-based formats such as Model UN, Mock Trial, Town Halls, and Public Comment, which mirror structures used in government. Discussion-based formats may also be familiar to many teachers, including Socratic Circles/Seminars or Structured Academic Controversy. These formats are distinct in that they often do not involve a "winner" in the debate and are more geared toward discussion to find consensus.

We have developed and adapted three competitive formats that offer the flexibility necessary to fit a debate into a limited classroom period with a large class, without the goal of necessarily preparing young people for competitions. These formats—Congress Debate, SPAR Debate, and Mini-Parliamentary Debate—can be adapted for different class sizes and amounts of time. They can be used across grade levels and subject areas, and any modifications depend primarily on choosing the topic for debate and its wording.

Congress Debate

The Congress Debate format is best when the goal is to have one debate that involves the entire class. It is helpful for students with disabilities and English language learners because it allows for more preparation time than other formats. In a Congress Debate, debaters may have as little as 15 minutes and as long as two weeks to research and prepare a speech advocating for a plan of action. The debate is about a policy topic, and debaters present solutions to an issue (either as solo presenters or in pairs). On the day of the debate, one person is the "presiding officer," calling on volunteers to speak and referring to them as "Senator/Representative [last name]." The debate continues in the "speech-questions-speech-questions" pattern until you or the presiding officer decide the debate is complete, after which there is a vote on which speech won the debate. This format is typically the only style of debate in which debaters choose their position. (See Figure 5.3 for more detail.)

SPAR Debate

A SPAR Debate is ideal when you want to teach the class to ask better questions and you want a simple way to help learners explore different perspectives in a short amount of time (see Figure 5.4 for more detail). SPAR stands for "Spontaneous Argumentation," and once the debate starts, debaters do not get additional preparation time. Although you can extend any of the times described in this protocol to increase rigor, the suggested timing generally results in an eight-minute debate that can fit nicely into many classroom periods. If running multiple debates, it is

FIGURE 5.3
Congress Debate Protocol

Steps	Task	Time (adjustable)
Prework	Teacher sets the debate topic or works with the class to do so, creates teams, names learners in the categories of "Representative" or "Senator," assigns a presiding officer, and teaches about argument structure for opening speeches and how to ask questions and create action plans.	Integrated into the content for the unit
Preparation time	Debaters work in teams or as individuals to prepare a 2- to 3-minute speech advocating for a plan of action on the side of their choosing.	15–20 minutes (or up to 2 weeks)
Opening speech	First group shares opening speech.	2–3 minutes
Cross-examination	Entire class (and/or outside guests) poses clarifying or probing questions as part of cross-examination.	1–2 minutes
Repeat	Everyone continues listening to speeches.	As long as available
Vote	Presiding officer calls for a vote on the issue.	1 minute
		Total: minimum of 22 minutes (including preparation), highly flexible based on how many speeches are presented

FIGURE 5.4
SPAR Debate Protocol

Steps	Task	Time (adjustable)
Prework	Teacher works with the class on argument structure, how to write an opening speech, and how to ask questions. Teacher announces a debate topic (or a choice of three) created by the teacher, debaters, or families. Teacher assigns groups and pro/con sides.	Integrated into the content for the unit
Preparation time	Debaters work in 1- to 3-person teams to prepare a 2-minute opening speech.	1–10 minutes
Affirmative (pro) opening speech	Affirmative (pro) team presents their opening speech.	1–2 minutes
Cross-examination	Entire class (and/or outside guests) poses clarifying or probing questions.	1 minute
Negative (con) opening speech	Negative (con) team presents their opening speech.	1–2 minutes
Cross-examination	Entire class (and/or outside guests) poses clarifying or probing questions.	1 minute
Negative (con) closing speech	Negative (con) team synthesizes the most important issues in the round and why they should win the debate.	30 seconds–1 minute
Affirmative (pro) closing speech	Affirmative (pro) team synthesizes the most important issues in the round and why they should win the debate.	30 seconds–1 minute

FIGURE 5.4
SPAR Debate Protocol (continued)

Steps	Task	Time (adjustable)
Reflection and feedback	Content and delivery feedback is given on the strongest arguments and examples of most persuasive delivery. Optional: Announce a winner based on class vote or rubric from the teacher.	5 minutes
		Total: 23 minutes maximum (can be shortened to 15 minutes with less preparation and written feedback)

good practice to give a new topic to each set of debaters so that they get to explore many different issues. You can save time by assigning all the topics at once and having everyone prepare at the same time. To reduce anxiety and make the experience more fun, many teachers use a Jeopardy board or spin a wheel to announce the topics. Because SPAR Debates are designed to be fast and simple, topics in the Fact category are best suited for this format.

Mini-Parliamentary Debate

Parliamentary Debate (known as "Parli") is a competitive form of debate used in high school and college debate tournaments and modeled after the British Parliament. It is a useful format for teaching young people to respond directly to arguments and synthesize complex conversations. It is also one of the only forms of debate that uses all types of topics—Fact, Value, and Policy—making it the easiest format to adapt for level of difficulty and types of content. We have adapted the competitive format with significantly shorter speech times, as a Mini-Parliamentary Debate, or Mini-Parli Debate (see Figure 5.5 for more detail).

As in SPAR, debaters work in small groups of two or three people after receiving a topic and being assigned their side. During preparation, debaters also figure out who will present during which speech, distributing time between all participants. Once the debate begins, there is no set time for questions; instead, speakers can interrupt opening speeches by raising their hand or standing up to ask questions, but only if the speaker accepts the question. The response sections of this protocol are the most "debatelike" of our three formats and require young people to learn how to structure arguments on the spot, anticipate and respond, and synthesize points. See Resources 8, 9, and 10 in The Practice Space's *Debate Guide* at www.practice-space.org/debate-guide for tips (Baines, 2020d).

FIGURE 5.5
Mini-Parliamentary Debate Protocol

Steps	Task	Time (adjustable)
Prework	Teacher works with the class on argument structure, how to write an opening speech, and how to come up with arguments on the spot. Teacher announces a debate topic (or a choice of three) that he or she creates or gets from the young people or families. Teacher assigns groups and assigns pro/con sides.	Integrated into the content for the unit
Preparation time	Debaters work in 2- to 3-person teams to prepare a 2-minute opening speech	10–20 minutes
Affirmative (pro) opening speech	Affirmative (pro) team presents their opening speech (with either one speaker or copresented).	3 minutes (including any questions asked throughout)

FIGURE 5.5
Mini-Parliamentary Debate Protocol (continued)

Steps	Task	Time (adjustable)
Negative (con) opening speech	Negative (con) team presents their opening speech (with either one speaker or copresented).	3 minutes (including any questions asked throughout)
Affirmative responses	Affirmative team responds to each of their opponent's points and also defends their own.	3 minutes
Negative responses	Negative team responds to each of their opponent's points and also defends their own.	3 minutes
Negative closing speech	Negative team synthesizes the most important issues in the round and why they should win the debate.	2 minutes
Affirmative closing speech	Affirmative team synthesizes the most important issues in the round and why they should win the debate.	2 minutes
Reflection and feedback	Content and delivery feedback is given on the strongest arguments and examples of most persuasive delivery. Optional: Announce a winner based on class vote or rubric from the teacher.	5 minutes
		Total: 41 minutes maximum (can be shortened to 20 minutes with 2-minute openings and responses and 1-minute closings, with written feedback)

Ensuring Adequate Preparation and Anticipating Struggle

It is common for young people to pull back and silence themselves if they get overwhelmed, confused, or have a bad initial experience speaking up. Adequate preparation for both listeners and speakers is key to helping your class maintain a growth mindset, focus on future improvement, and struggle productively. Depending on learners' backgrounds and histories, debate can be an immediately fun, gamelike activity, or it can be a stressful, high-stakes opportunity to defend their most important viewpoints and advocate for themselves. To make debate an equitable experience, it is essential to remember that not everyone comes to debate with the same lens and to anticipate possible struggles.

Supporting the Debate Mindset

Practice is important to help young people gain confidence with debate and improve their skills, which takes time and repetition with quality feedback. Doing more short debates on a variety of topics is better than doing one long debate on a single topic. Also, longer debates should happen only if the students have participated in shorter debates and been able to fill the shorter speech times with appropriate content.

Adapting the debate formats to integrate them into your lessons as formative assessments and warm-ups can help young people develop their skills to analyze both sides of an issue, outline quickly, listen, take notes, synthesize, explain, and extend their thinking (see Resource 5 in The Practice Space's *Debate Guide* [Baines, 2020d] at www.practice-space .org/debate-guide). According to 16-year-old Ava Acosta, "Debate helps you prepare your reasons, be concise, and summarize. It helps your public speaking because it organizes your thoughts."

To prepare learners for a successful debate experience, spend time reframing the purpose of debate and why it is both fun and important in life. Unearth inaccurate assumptions about what debate is (e.g., fighting or shouting). As you gradually introduce and prepare debates, emphasize the importance of staying current and being aware of conversations in the world, especially as a way to anticipate arguments and prepare in a short amount of time. During more complex debates, it can also be useful to offer opportunities for young people to teach one another and run their own "Topic Analysis Seminars" to share what they know about topics and practice asking questions.

For most young people, learning to debate both sides of an issue is one of the most challenging aspects of debate. It is also key to reaping benefits such as perspective taking and developing empathy and understanding of different viewpoints and identities. Consider these observations of 17-year-old Jacob Klein:

> One of the most important things about debate is that it introduces you to new perspectives. The opinions of children in my experience tend to be almost always the same as their parents or are strongly motivated by society and the things around them. By researching and discussing both sides, you as the debater are now able to come to your own conclusion about where your opinion lies. Even when I don't win the round (actually, especially when I don't win the round), I am able to learn so much about a topic that I hadn't ever really thought of. It can truly alter the student's perspective, challenging their assumptions about society, providing them with tools they can use to form opinions on other topics. Debate is truly life-changing in terms of what it can do to developing minds.

Warm-Ups to Practice Skills

Although debate can be deeply impactful, this outcome is something that happens over time and not in a single debate. If full debates are overwhelming, try starting with warm-up drills and "debate-light" activities such as This or That, 20 Questions, Justify It, or Take Action. See Resource 13 in The Practice Space's *Debate Guide* (Baines, 2020d) at www.practice-space.org/debate-guide for more detail.

This or That. In addition to its use in storytelling described in Chapter 4, this icebreaker helps address the common struggle to commit to an argument. Binary prompts are posed (e.g., hot or cold, savory or sweet, animals or plants), and each person has to explain his or her choice.

20 Questions. This fun game involves the class asking closed yes or no questions to try to guess the person, place, or object that another classmate has in mind. The goal is to lower anxiety around asking questions.

Justify It. This activity introduces argument structure, with one person choosing and stating a claim, such as "Gorillas would make great pets," followed by the next person adding a reason why, and the next person saying why it all matters.

Take Action. In this activity, the class brainstorms societal problems and records them on index cards. Learners draw cards at random and have to state a solution to the problem, which gives them practice in spontaneous speaking skills.

Light-touch activities can help lower stress around public speaking over time and offer an entry point to young people who have typically felt silenced or have had challenges participating or thinking of what to say. See Figure 5.6 for common struggles and possible support mechanisms.

FIGURE 5.6
Issues and Supports

Common Debate Issue	Suggested Support
Not having prior knowledge about a topic or having trouble coming up with initial ideas	Provide an overview sheet on the topic, have a brief class discussion, or tell personal stories related to the topic. Begin with topics closer to the students' own experience.
Defending a side that is different from personal beliefs	Work alongside the group to help them explore the other side's perspective and find an angle or a way of defining key terms so that they don't directly contradict beliefs.
Preparing the wrong side	At the start of preparation time, check in with groups to make sure sides are correct.

FIGURE 5.6
Issues and Supports (continued)

Common Debate Issue	Suggested Support
Teamwork issues (e.g., one person dominating the preparation)	Have people take turns sharing their initial thoughts (timed at 1 minute each). Assign a facilitator role to make sure everyone gets a chance to share, and give everyone checklists for what needs to get done.
Speeches that are too short and lack elaboration and impacts	While monitoring preparation or giving feedback, focus on making sure debaters offer support for each of their points and say why the points matter.
Not asking questions	Post sentence-starters for questions or have debaters prepare them in advance.
Not structuring the points presented	Post a template for opening speeches, having debaters label "My first contention is . . . ," "My second contention is . . . ," and so on.
Scattered ideas and disorganized responses	Make sure debaters say which argument they are responding to (e.g., "They say . . . I say . . .").
Missing the other side's arguments	Teach debaters how to take quick outline notes, not writing every detail down or using full sentences, but using abbreviations and noting only key points.
Not knowing how to come up with arguments on the spot	During preparation, help debaters anticipate what the other side might say and what they might say back.
Not knowing how to end	Use the go-to debate conclusion phrase for speech endings: "For all these reasons, we urge you to vote in favor of . . . ."

Teaching Learners How to Listen

Listening is the skill that debate can teach better than any other activity. Without strong listening skills, it is impossible to participate in a debate, take up new perspectives to use in succeeding rounds, give feedback and learn from it, or collaborate with teammates. Like many other things, listening takes practice and guidance. When it comes to debate, preparing young people as listeners means offering them the opportunity to judge, coach, and give feedback.

When having the class judge debates, coconstruct norms that remind them to clear away their biases and rely only on the arguments presented in the debate round. Norms can also include looking encouraging (e.g., nodding) and taking notes. When announcing decisions, listeners should give feedback on both the content and the delivery of the arguments and justify their decisions. Doing so may require some modeling and simulated practice to help people get away from comments like "You stuttered too much" and instead offer more substantive observations about which arguments were strongest and why, and why they were persuaded by someone's delivery. Give student judges a rubric or a checklist of focus areas of feedback. Make sure they identify what each side did well, not just what they could have done better. These practices help young people share power in the classroom and also push back against dominant and oppressive public speaking norms. For more tips on listening, see Resource 6 in The Practice Space's *Debate Guide* (Baines, 2020d) at www.practice-space.org/debate-guide.

Tips for the Teacher's Role

The role of the teacher shifts in the context of debate. Although debate requires teacher-led guidance at the beginning, it can gradually become an almost entirely youth-led activity. Over time, the role of the teacher in facilitating debates becomes more about timing speeches, guiding the topic writing and selection, giving prompts and reminders, and being the cheerleader. The structure is especially comforting for young people who are English language learners or who have never spoken up in class before. Instead of feeling put on the spot, they can view debate as a predictable structure that helps them know what to expect—even if what they are expecting is to have to speak spontaneously. By anticipating struggles and putting additional support in place, the teacher plays an important role in scaffolding voice.

Beyond facilitation, the teacher also helps offer formative feedback to help learners improve and persist. According to 16-year-old Mercy Niyi-Awolesi,

> The advice I would give to teachers who are starting to use debate in their classroom is to provide in-depth feedback. Feedback is very essential in learning because it is the key to improvement and progress. It also gives students confidence and it promotes a growth mindset.

Both teacher and student should understand that the goal of a formative-feedback activity is not to achieve a "perfect" debate or demonstrate mastery of key skills, but to practice key skills and improve them—in the same way that serious runners do not run to show an audience how fast they are, but to become stronger. When giving feedback, it helps to prioritize a few key debate-related skills and announce them as the focus. These can include separate content- and delivery-oriented focus areas such as these:

- Organization
- Clarity
- Use of examples
- Reasoning
- Voice (volume, tone, modulation)
- Physicality (gestures, eye contact, facial expressions)

Incorporating these areas into a rubric that is cocreated with the class can help learners become involved in the assessment process, and the rubric can also be used for self-assessment or peer assessment after debates. To adapt for different grade levels, rubrics can incorporate illustrations or images at the lower end, or they can provide for more in-depth assessment at the upper end by including a greater number of elements, with boxes for written comments. More ambitious projects, such as a week-long debate tournament with multiple debate rounds, can also include these same cocreated rubrics as comment sheets for outside judges. For an example, see Resource 16 in The Practice Space's *Debate Guide* (Baines, 2020d) at www.practice-space.org/debate-guide.

Final Takeaways

To sum up the guidance provided in this chapter, one of our debaters, 16-year-old Ava Acosta, outlines the following five tips for teachers:

1. Provide students with a clear outline of the debate structure and useful sites where they can look up reliable and helpful information.
2. Students should make mistakes in order to learn and do better.
3. If you are having debates or debate events, come up with a theme so that topics can be centered around it. It would give a sense of organization.
4. Making sure everyone is comfortable is really essential. Calm, collected students tend to perform better than those who are anxious and overly scared (I can speak from experience). I think the best way to avoid this would be just to prepare. Prior to events, have students practice actual debates or have timed sessions where they have to research a given topic in x minutes. Personally, finding evidence is my weakest point, so doing this type of exercise would be best.
5. All of this sounds so meticulous and tedious, but I promise it is worth it! Whether it be talking on the spot or being able to research quick, credible facts, there is never a dull moment. Debate is always going to be a learning experience and mainly because you will truly never know what comes next. That is its true beauty.

Yes, Ava, indeed it is.

6

Poetry to Spark Conversation

Of Tears in Class

We were "popcorn reading"
in 4th period English class.
It was the final chapter
of Steinbeck's classic book
about the mice and the men.
Stuff went down in the story.

Poor Lenny and his homie George
were heading towards a reckoning.

As I waited for my turn to read
I traced names of taggers and cholitos
who carved themselves into the surface
of the wood desk where I was sitting.

My fingers were so fascinated by these
hood hieroglyphics I lost track of the story.

My turn came. I read the passage
it moved me with talk of rivers and dreams.
Until one homie shot the other in the back.
I started crying and blinking.
My tears fell on the page like raindrops.

One classmate mumbled, "Yo, she's crying!"
Then the whole class started to laugh at me.
"It's just a book" someone else shouted
The teacher tried but failed
to hold in his laughter, "Are you ok?"
I said, "No. This is sad."

We were reading about friends
and grief and we weren't going to talk about it?
We weren't going to ponder this tragedy?

I wondered why my tears were not as welcome
as my classmates' laughter about them.

I felt for Lenny, for his loss of agency
for the sprinkles of intolerance that
plagued him throughout this whole book.
I understood what that felt like but
there was no space for those thoughts now.

The teacher didn't acknowledge my tears
but thanked me for my "enthusiasm"
about the story while I wiped my face.
We never talked about what happened.
For the rest of the year, I was
known as "the girl who cried in English class"
I don't know if it was an insult or a compliment.
It always felt like a little of both.

—Diana Medina

There is no braver space than a space where poetry is shared and performed. In these spaces, individuals show up not only to share their own work but to witness others doing the same. Poetry is an art form that can be emotional, combative, melancholy, or joyful, depending on the poet. Just like debate, poetry explores clash, contradictions, pros, cons, and morality. The difference is that in poetry, an individual is having those conversations internally in order to produce written art or a moving performance.

Poetry can provide an opportunity for young people to articulate their feelings, share them with others, and name what they are seeing happening in the world. For this chapter, we interviewed seven poets ranging in age from 18 to 75. They come from all over the United States, have had their works published, and have a variety of jobs, including student, educator, bureaucrat, comedian, and scientist. They are skilled public speakers whose connection to poetry showcases how to share ideas from a place of authenticity.

Poetry as an Educational Tool

Poetry is the practice of reaching into oneself to pull out feelings, energies, burdens, and pains and describing them vividly. Poetry allows us to attach words to emotions, paint pictures with sentences, and use our own voice to name common yet intangible parts of what it means to be human.

Young people have this gift in abundance and a deep desire to use it, whether they say so or not. The unique offering of poetry is its ability to serve as a catalyst for conversations. When it is performed, it gives listeners an opportunity to feel, think, and witness. In this way, poetry creates spaces where all of us can become both a learner and a teacher. It invites us to engage in debates with ourselves over who we are, what we think, how we want to show up in the world, and what we need from others.

Spoken-word poetry is an expressive and artistic form of public speaking that can be used to spark conversations about human experiences by isolating specific moments, honoring diverse styles, and attaching words to emotions. When poetry is on the page, it can be read, dissected, discussed, and analyzed. When poetry is on the stage (or shared out loud), speakers make choices about how their worlds can be embodied and animated, and this invites others who may be feeling the same way to share. Poetry is the personification of what happens when public speaking is done as an act of liberation: an ability to share a story, tell a truth, have distance from one's pains, and still make them heard to reinvent them.

Poetry can support many academic objectives: to identify themes, interpret words and phrases, and analyze meaning. The missed opportunity is that poetry can be so much more. It can be a way to welcome voices and perspectives that look and sound like the young people we teach or to make space for them to respond creatively to themes in academic content. Poetry is not just a source of informational text that can be analyzed in an English class. It is also a source of inspirational text that can deepen learning and move learners to create, speak, and be heard. Building a culture of connection and fostering equity in classrooms is more important than ever—and poetry can play a role in building that culture. What is important to remember is that poetry can serve multiple purposes and reinforce many things that are already happening in the classroom while adding the layer of connection and expression.

There are many benefits of poetry:

- Builds speaking, reading, and listening skills
- Develops language and vocabulary
- Improves critical thinking
- Connects to culture and self-exploration
- Stimulates brainstorming and creative thinking
- Builds a love for reading and storytelling
- Promotes empathy, community building, and peer connections
- Builds confidence through defining inner voice
- Helps English language learners build language skills
- Builds resilience and fosters social and emotional learning
- Explores all aspects of life and society

Poetry's Roots in Oral Traditions

Poetry is historically rooted in oral traditions. Long before society had the technology of the printing press, history and stories were shared orally in easy-to-remember verses and phrases to be passed on. In this way, the practice of poetry is more than just an art form; it is a connection to something deeply ancestral. In precolonial times, poetry was a cornerstone of African societies. It was part of politics, ceremony, spiritual practice, and entertainment. One could easily argue that it was the Twitter or TikTok of the time.

Poetry is deeply entrenched in the need to reclaim power. It has been used not only as a device to connect and inform but as a method of resistance. The bilingual poetry collection *Resistencia: Poems of Protest and Revolution* (Eisner & Escaja, 2020) discusses how in the Americas there is a deep and vibrant history of a "poetry of witness." According to Julia Alvarez, who wrote the book's introduction, "often all that was left to the powerless was the power of testimony; the only rebellion possible was that of the rebel word" (p. xvii). In this way, poetry ensured the powerless were not forgotten or ignored. Using poetry, people have protested imperialism, dictatorships, injustice, and economic inequality while also leaning into the strength of their collective identities.

In the United States, spoken-word poetry was a powerful mechanism that fueled the movements of many marginalized groups seeking to resist and name the oppression they experienced from the powers that be. Poets were at the center, using poetry as a means to name injustice, express lived experiences, and speak truth to power. Lori Walkington (2020) studied the connections between spoken-word poetry and social justice in San Diego communities for her paper "Speak About It, Be About It: Spoken-Word Poetry Communities and Transformative Social Justice." She notes, "'Spoken-word poetry' and the knowledge we can gain from the poets who perform it are integral to the successful recovery of members of oppressed communities" (p. 649). Poetry is used as an attempt to resist, shape thinking, and challenge systems while still trying to exist within them.

Poetry and social justice movements work hand in hand. Recently there have been uprisings in various cities in the United States in response to the ongoing killing of Black people at the hands of police. In response, young people were reading poems at rallies and sharing poems of pain and frustration on social media. One of them even got the opportunity to read her poem at a presidential inauguration. At this moment, all over the world, young people are grappling with issues of fairness, bias, discrimination, and justice. Internally, they are grappling with a different set of challenges around identity, belonging, and becoming. Poet Audre

Lorde (2020) said it best: "It is through poetry that we give name to those ideas which are—until the poem—nameless and formless, about to be birthed, but already felt" (p. 3).

"The Hill We Climb" and the Power of Poetry

At age 22, Amanda Gorman was the youngest poet to speak at a presidential inauguration. After four tumultuous years under the Trump administration and the rollercoaster of 2020, Gorman had plenty of material to write a scathing critical poem. It could have been dark, angry, or even dystopian. Instead, her poem, "The Hill We Climb," wove together her story with messages of hope, gentle challenges, and invitations to ponder who we want to be as a country. In one line she states, "Being American is more than a pride we inherit—It's the past we step into and how we repair it." Delivered in a rhythmic cadence garnished with smiles and hand gestures, her poem didn't shy away from naming the dark things we had experienced, but she juxtaposed them with broader concepts to ponder. Upon its conclusion, with the audience clapping and nodding, it was clear this moment was history in the making.

The most interesting part of the performance was the conversations her poem sparked on television and other news outlets in the following days. Replays of Gorman reciting her poem had pundits and talk show hosts engaging with poetry instead of their typically combative crosstalk-style debates. Panels of talking heads went line by line through her piece, relating choices of words and feelings evoked, and sharing what it made them think about. During an interview on *The Daily Show* with Trevor Noah, Gorman said the intention of her piece was to "use words to go back to the quintessence of what America can be." As a country, we were in a moment where one young Black woman's poetic expression served as a much-needed mirror to help us see ourselves. It was a powerful catalyst to spark healing from the collective trauma of a pandemic, a message of hope for people of color recovering from the white supremacist antics of the last administration, and a reminder that there is still more work to be done.

Equity Through Poetry

Poetry has always been part of the curriculum and standards of English language arts. Poets such as Walt Whitman, Robert Frost, and Emily Dickinson are among the few anointed by academic literati. Maybe some students get a sprinkle of Maya Angelou or Langston Hughes as part of a Black History Month lesson.

To promote equity and move beyond the traditional and predictable choices, we can look to voices outside the chosen few for poetic inspiration, tapping into song lyrics, young poets who post or perform on social media, lines from favorite TV shows, and news headlines. A Sacramento-based poet notes that a simple way to begin this process is to invite young people to help find poetry in the voices they already listen to. He suggests:

> Work together to make a list of the songs they are listening to right now. There is already poetry in the lyrics of songs they like. Work with them to break down the lyrics in the songs. Ask, what is the who, what, when, where, and why? What devices are they using? What metaphors are present? Don't shy away from some of the words, themes or topics that feel uncomfortable. It can create meaningful conversations.

These voices can and should be taught alongside the classics, and young people know where to find them, if you ask. Poetry offers the ability to harness a kind of intelligence that involves learning from stories and voices of people who are capturing modern history as it is happening now.

Affirming Learners' Expertise and Worth

Accessing young people's funds of knowledge starts with affirming that they are experts in their own life. They have opinions worthy of being shared. They have a community and space where they can say what is on their mind out loud. Making space for expression fully honors the symbiotic relationship that exists between intellect and emotions. As multifaceted beings, all people must master this dance, and young people need practice doing so in spaces that support this aspect of their development.

Author, poet, and educator Alejandra Ramos Gómez notes that poetry is a powerful support in building classroom culture because of the ownership it provides students as they express their learnings in new ways. This effect will ripple out to other content areas. She offers the following recommendations:

> Take examples of other youth around the world. For instance, the Malala Foundation's newsletter includes poetry and writings by youth from around the world. They're really good. They're usually about global goals, climate, and all of these things. I think that's really useful to see kids who are doing that because many of our students, especially if they're students from underserved communities, don't see it as possible. They don't see themselves in those spaces. So just showing them that there are actually [young] people talking about these things, people from your community. And open the idea for them that if there's not someone, then that might be you. You do have the power to do that, to be the first one who speaks for your community or where you come from.

Poetry and Intersectionality

Intersectionality and poetry are deeply linked. Many poets—from Langston Hughes, Maya Angelou, and Audre Lorde to lesser-known, local poets—use their writing to shed light on the complexity of their identities. As one of our authors, Diana Medina, reflects:

> I began writing poetry to make sense of the confusion I felt as a female, bilingual, bicultural, first-generation Mexican American. I didn't know how to manage the tension I felt between the conflicting messages I received at home about the role of women in a family and society and the messages I got from teachers at school and television telling me I could be anything I wanted. I needed to put words to the struggle I felt trying to speak to my parents in Spanish when all of the thoughts in my brain were in English. I often wondered why it was that we spoke the same language and yet we couldn't ever find a common understanding. Poetry gave me an outlet to explore those layers within myself, the root

of each of those struggles, and name the ways they were weighing heavy on my heart.

Encouraging students to read poems with an intersectional lens before engaging in their own writing can guide those who are processing the impacts of their intersecting identities in the world. These types of poems can also show students the many ways authenticity can look and sound. The beauty of poetry is in the way it encourages playing with language and welcoming the use of rhythms. Poetry gives writers permission to decide what they want to say and how they want to say it. All students deserve to have choice in their expression while speaking their truth on their own creative terms.

Many educators see taking the time to teach learners how to speak and listen authentically as an afterthought in favor of academics. An emphasis on test scores creates urgency to get through content, with little room for creativity. This dynamic in the typical U.S. classroom results in a situation where the perception of who is smart or a good student is predicated on a young person's ability to play by the rules, often forgoing authentic expression in the process. Add to this dynamic the ongoing struggles of students of color, low-income students, English language learners, first-generation students, and students living through trauma and we have a perfect storm of young people being silenced. If school can only be a safe haven for young people when they are willing to follow rigid rules of engagement, when do they get to learn the skills they need to have agency in their own liberation?

Getting Started

The first and most important step in building your poetic toolbox is to start within. Do you have a favorite poem or song lyric? Is it something you can share with your students? Poetry will thrive in an environment where connection is present. Connection cannot happen if the facilitators of that environment (the educators) do not show their humanity.

Poet and teaching artist Len Germinara reinforces this point. He advises, "Start with work and poetry that resonates with you: If you don't like it, they won't like it." Using poetry as a teaching tool and vehicle for youth expression begins with understanding its connection to emotions firsthand. By engaging in writing prompts along with young people, you can model how to make those connections. A good question to ask yourself is "Where in my lessons is there room for exploring emotions as part of learning?"

Here are some ways to get started with introducing poetry in the classroom:

- **Start with one-word themes.** Pick a word of the day (maybe one connected to a content element or concept you will cover later) and have learners write an acrostic poem (in which the first letter in each line spells out a word or phrase).
- **Create a simple framework.** Use a simple writing framework to inspire open-ended writing, such as choosing a color, an emotion, and a place, and create a poem from that; or give a scope to each stanza, such as one stanza about the past, one stanza about the present, and one stanza about the future.
- **Set a timer.** Set a timer for five to eight minutes—enough time to stay in brainstorming mode and put some ideas on paper but not enough to allow overthinking. When time is limited, the first things that come to mind tend to be the most authentic, unfiltered thoughts. Learners can then come back to these thoughts to create a more developed poem.
- **Set a line goal.** Encourage students to write a certain number of lines. These lines can just be a series of random thoughts about a theme or word; they don't even need to be complete sentences. As students build comfort with this process, increase the number of lines they write (eventually you can have the line goal become a stanza goal); for example, have them write two stanzas of four lines each, with each stanza focused on exploring one element of a theme or an idea.

- **Follow the format of an existing poem.** Introduce a poem by another poet and have students follow that stanza or line structure. This approach demystifies the writing process because the existing poem provides sentence-starters that students can use to insert their own thoughts.

Cultivate a Poetic Mindset

Beyond the starting points just described, cultivating a "poetic mindset" can broaden the opportunities for bringing poetry into your classroom. A poetic mindset drives where and how you find inspiration and see the poetry in the world around you. Here are some tips and concepts to cultivate this mindset:

- **Change the environment.** Move desks, sit in circles, go outside. A new sense of place, facing a new direction in the room, sitting in a different seat, or feeling sunshine or wind before creating poetry will help open up expression and creativity.
- **Recognize that if they are our words, they are poetry.** What makes something poetic is the poet. Contrary to popular belief, poems do not have to rhyme (though some do). Poems just have to speak the truth. Whether we know it or not, all of us speak in poetry.
- **Play the "that's a poem" game.** Searching for poetry prompts is easy if we are looking all around us. Our favorite song lyric: that's a poem. A comment a student makes about hating peas: that's a poem. A sentence in a textbook: that's a poem. Prompts are just the starting point; the poetry can flow from there.
- **Realize that everything has layers: the ones we see and the ones that we create.** Every moment and situation is layered, depending on where we put our focus. From the clothing we wear to the identities we have, layers are everywhere. Pick one and write about it.
- **Go on metaphor scavenger hunts.** This activity is a great way to lean into mindfulness while remaining open to inspiration. Every situation can be a metaphor for something else, whether it be driving a car, writing with a pencil, or even finding a lost shoe.

- **Engage all the senses.** Poetry is about painting a picture with words. The best way to do that is to bring all the senses to the party and connect them in unexpected ways. For instance, what does the color red taste like? How does it feel? Does it sound like anything?
- **Have conversations with things.** This exercise takes the idea of personification one step further by inviting us to have conversations with things around us. For example, what does a conversation with our shoes sound like? If they could speak, what would they say and how would we respond?

When engaging in exercises such as these, remember that the goal is to inspire thinking and just write. Expression-Driven Teaching values unfinished expression-in-progress. So remind your students to let go of perfection and not edit themselves. No poem is ever finished. It is OK if it sounds one way today and a different way tomorrow.

Step Out of Comfort Zones

The most important aspect of introducing poetry in the classroom is the willingness to listen and be open to new ideas. It's important to not devalue other forms or styles that appeal to young people. Remember that poetry can help them connect to societal issues and concerns. It is OK to read outside a curriculum and for students to speak up about what poetry they want to read in class.

What is valuable is the learning journey poetry can provide. For instance, looking to news sources as poetic inspiration can be a way for young people to consider how systems of power work, where power resides, or how power is communicated to the rest of society. The power in creating poetry together is that it creates a space where everyone learns something, everyone teaches something, and everyone is seen and witnessed in an organic and authentic community.

Lastly, remember this: there's a poem for everyone. There's a poem that is perfect for your classroom if you are willing to dig, work with your students to find it, and take a few steps out of your comfort zone.

Use Poetry Beyond English Language Arts

Poetry can be a catalyst to stimulate expression and discussion in topics beyond English language arts. In history, for example, poetry can be a great way to explore the sentiments and issues of a particular era. Poetry can be a primary source to gauge the emotions of people at a certain time; learners can then engage in poetic responses that highlight similar emotions with creative performance elements. Poetry can add depth to the content conveyed in a chapter of a history book or a presidential speech as part of the same unit.

You can also explore mathematical concepts via poetry. Both rely on metaphor and explanation. In math, we substitute variables and symbols for numbers. We see different perspectives on two sides of an equal sign and say they are an analogy for each other in order to solve it. In this way, all equations are metaphors. Equations can be explored with poetry as a fun way to create a goal other than getting a right answer—for instance, creating poetic equations as a warm-up discussion prompt such as "Love = Place/People." A prompt like this helps bring attention to the concept that mathematics symbols have concrete meaning, while stimulating discussions about individual experiences or serving as inspiration for students to create their own poetic equations.

Even the sciences present many opportunities to connect with poetry. Sarah Oktay, a poet with a PhD in chemical oceanography, notes:

> Poetry often is one of the best ways to communicate things we don't understand or things that are mystical or spiritual or weird or alien. I think it's a really helpful way. Really poetry is the only way you can describe some of these things. There is intense beauty associated with the ocean and also kind of big feelings of how small we are in the universe or what we don't know. It's pitch black so you're exploring with just a flashlight. In effect we're having to get all of our information from instruments. So there's a layer of magic almost between us and what we're measuring.

Oktay believes that young people speak in poetry naturally. For 12 years, she ran a nature exploration program in Nantucket, Massachusetts, for 10th and 11th graders from Boston. It included a poetry component rooted in *ecopoetics*, the use of poetic texts and the creation of poetry with a strong emphasis on environments and nature. The program helped young people articulate their reactions to nature as they observed it, many for the first time. Oktay continues, "It was perfect for them because it gave them a construct to put their feelings and their thoughts and get their ideas out. It's a lot easier to use poetry [than to write a] paragraph or an essay."

Poetry as Inspiration and Expression of Emotion

Poetry is deeply aligned with social and emotional learning because it helps us learn more about ourselves and how we relate to the world around us. When shared under the right conditions, poetry helps us make meaning and recognize connections.

Looking to poetry as a source of inspirational text can open up many possibilities for learning and engagement, particularly in subjects that young people might struggle to connect with. Using analysis techniques that students are already learning, such as close reading, is a great way to connect to poetry. When learners engage in close reading of an informational text, they are looking for significant details or patterns that can help them gauge conclusions or make meaning. Engaging in intentional close reading of a poem (whether one you provide or one their classmates created) can help learners see how emotions are conveyed and encourage them to connect it with details from their life. You can also take this activity a step further by encouraging students to identify a line that resonates with them from a text and use that as the first line of their poem. Framing poetry as inspirational text gives young people choice in how it can be reinvented to become relevant to their current contexts. For elementary students, poetry can also help support reading development and inspire them to begin connecting words with feelings. For example, a core standard for 5th graders is being able to portray the tone of a word and the meaning of a word through art. One poet had success using a playful exercise called "chain-link poetry," in which students create word displays on big pieces of cardboard that can be hung on a fence. The students help "design" each word by writing it and coloring it in a manner that illustrates how the word might feel to them. Students then can play a game creating their own poems by combining the words in different ways.

Viewing Poetry as a Frame for Creativity and Emotion

When framed properly, poetry can help young people process their emotions as they figure out who they are becoming. Poetry offers a layered experience for the speaker and the listener alike. As former U.S. poet laureate Billy Collins (2005) put it, "To hear a poem is to experience its momentary escape from the prison cell of the page, where silence is enforced, to a freedom dependent only on the ability to open the mouth—the most democratic of instruments—and speak" (p. 3). Spoken-word poetry is an expressive and artistic form of public speaking that sparks conversation about human experiences by isolating specific moments and honoring diverse styles. From the standpoint of social and emotional learning, spoken-word poetry can be a powerful tool to give voice to students' inner struggles, emotions, and thoughts. These moments of expression are when they make important decisions about who they will be and how they will show up in the world.

The exploration of expression through poetry happens on two levels: the creation of the poem and the performance. In this way, preparation and conceptualization are just as important as tone and presentation. All of these become an invitation for a young person to feel. Having the permission to feel, a method to reflect, and a way to unburden emotions playfully and passionately can be incredibly healing. The mindful exercise of exploring unedited thoughts using the coded language of similes, metaphors, or word choice makes social and emotional learning come to life.

Bringing Emotions to Light via Nonjudgmental Writing

The process of moving from childhood to adolescence to adulthood is internally grueling because of the evolution that it asks of us. For young people, having an outlet such as poetry to engage with as part of their ongoing evolution can be truly transformative. Poetry offers a place for students to engage in nonjudgmental writing, to reflect creatively about themselves, decide who they are becoming, name their convictions, and decide how they want to use their voice to show themselves to the world. According to an Indiana-based poet, author, and educator, the process starts with emptying out what is on the mind. She states:

> I don't try to write a poem. I just write. Then I start seeing some potential there, but I'm not trying to write a poem. My mindset is just empty. Don't worry. I don't worry about spelling. I don't worry about grammar. I don't worry about my sentence structure, which was really hard for me in the beginning. Just empty out, just pour out and then see what comes.

She frames this emptying process in the same way for her students:

> I really feel like when my students write poetry, they know they're not being judged. They know it's something from them. A lot of them just love and enjoy doing it. When they are able to share that part of them-selves, that, too, helps overcome fears.

Poetry, when it is written or performed, is a powerful antidote that can disrupt the stressors in our lives, stressors that many of us learn to endure and survive without naming them. Poetry provides a proper out-let to release, transform, or reinvent them, which is both part of its allure and part of why people find it intimidating.

The process of emptying what is on a young person's mind can be challenging to do without a starting point to stimulate thinking. One way to support this process of emptying out thoughts is to engage in guided brainstorming before writing a poem. Here are some examples:

- List five of your favorite hobbies. Choose one hobby on that list. Write a poem about the first time your hands discovered that hobby.
- List three truths about the world. List three things that people think about you that are not true. Write a poem about an inconvenient truth inspired by one of your lists.
- List five words that come to mind when you hear the word [insert a one-word theme]. Write a poem that uses two of the words you listed.

Using Poetic Performance to Embody Emotions

In the delivery of poetry, body language and facial expressions are just as important as words. Before poetry becomes public speaking, it begins as a conversation with self. Performing a poem requires individuals to explore themselves, make meaning of inner thoughts, and decide how those thoughts will be expressed nonverbally. Additionally, the energy of the audience and their response are also important. What makes a poem come to life is sharing it with others. Each time it is shared, it can feel different or be changed. The speaker has creative choice in what is said and how it is said through the use of voice and body. All of these choices also inform the experience of the listener.

So where should young people begin when wanting to take a poetic idea off the page and into an embodied performance? Poet and actor Ike Torres recommends looking to music for inspiration. He states, "I know the material, like a musician would know their notes. I know how to play the scales. I have that locked into memory. I'm able to go with the flow, figure out what the crowd is lacking within two minutes, and get a feel for what's effective and what's not." In this way, preparing through an outline still applies, just as in other methods of public speaking or academic writing. The difference is that the outline shows the performance choices that the person will make in the poem and allows space for adaptation in the moment. Torres continues, "I want to be talking to the audience, but I also want the audience to talk to me. We're creating harmony together."

Teaching Learners How to Listen

Because poetry can make its creators feel incredibly vulnerable, it must be paired with active and intentional listening. In spaces such as open mics, facilitators use certain norms to show poets they are being heard and to affirm them. Such tactics can easily be added to the listening norms of a classroom. Here are two examples:

- **Snaps and Silent Applause.** Listeners snap their fingers or use the American Sign Language sign for applause (hands at sides with fingers spread out) while a poet is reading to show appreciation for a line, applaud a word choice, or signal agreement without adding noise.

- **Giving Flowers.** Individuals take turns verbally congratulating and complimenting a poet after the performance. This practice gives listeners the chance to affirm the poet by naming things they liked, felt, or deeply resonated with. They can also express thanks for the poet's courage if the poem covered a topic that was hard to bring up or risked vulnerability. (Note: This interaction is different from feedback.)

As the last part of the Giving Flowers option suggests, it is important to help students develop their listening skills in a way that promotes compassion, care, and respect for their peers' experiences. A useful sentence frame for responding to a poem is "When you said [insert word/phrase], it made me think of [insert what came to mind]." This frame guides students to listen for specific phrases or word choices in a poem so they are able to respond thoughtfully. They can insert whatever comes to mind, including a similar experience, a visual, or a place. This tactic is effective because it goes beyond general positive feedback such as "I liked it" or "It was good" and instead invites students to listen for what resonates.

Feedback

As with other modalities of expression, providing feedback to students who write and share poetry can support their growth as writers and speakers. The most important thing to do when facilitating feedback on student poetry is to separate this process from the sharing process. Sometimes the act of sharing a piece of poetry requires so much vulnerability from learners that the idea of also being critiqued on it can create more fear or anxieties. We recommend calling the time you provide feedback a "workshop" so that students know that it is a space designed to help them grow their poetry-writing skills. Then, students can opt in to receiving feedback and select a piece they would like feedback on. Once this designated space is created, the feedback you offer should include the following elements:

- **Uplifting and affirming word choices** that are creative or powerful.
- **Questions to push thinking** on subject matter or to encourage clarifying an idea; for example, "What did you mean by [insert word choice]?" or "What else can you say about [insert topic]?"
- **Sharing your experience as a reader and listener** of the poem, including naming the specific things you liked (e.g., repetition, detail, tone) and things you wanted to hear more about.
- **Sharing what left you wondering.** This can help learners add more to their pieces and is a particularly helpful type of feedback for those who may feel stuck on a poem they would like to finish.
- **Asking someone other than the writer to read a poem** so the writer can hear the work in a different person's voice and reflect on it. This element can also promote community building and mutual support, as reading another person's poem must be approached with great care and trust.

Final Takeaways

Ultimately, bringing poetry into the classroom can create learning opportunities that are powerful, playful, creative, and deeply transformative. Sacramento-based poet and student Chianne "Cloudy" Rhodes Carrier states:

> I think it's important to start with what poetry was. The old white man poetry to be exact, the classics, Shakespeare's sonnets, all those things. But then teach about spoken word poetry and where that was birthed from. How it was birthed from people of color and how it was born in ancient Greece, when men just wanted to get up on a stage and tell their story. It should have an evolution to it that is theatrical

because that's what keeps kids engaged. When they know that it has been all these different things, it's worn all these jackets, it's worn all these hats and it's become all these different things than you as students, you can make it something new. It's still changing.

We couldn't agree more, Cloudy.

7

Presentation and Listening to Express Authenticity

Expressing emotions, opinions, and experiences takes incredible courage and a willingness to be a bit different. For a young person in a classroom full of judgmental peers, the pressure to erase individuality is palpable, especially for someone who just wants to be accepted and loved. When faced with standing at the front of a room to give a presentation, it is easier to shrink from the spotlight, keeping a carefully blank face, reading off slides, hands in pockets, avoiding the risk that any gestures will look even remotely strange. The experience of giving a presentation is often seared into the mind of the speaker (especially for those who intensely dread public speaking), and yet, most presentations are barely memorable to those who listen to them.

Classroom presentations too often sound exactly the same, when they should be a tool for educating and inspiring interest. This situation parallels the professional world, where presentations are one of the most common methods for expressing ideas and information—and are also incredibly dull. The best presentations stand out because the speakers have taken a risk with their ideas as well as how they have chosen to structure and deliver them.

Whereas debate is about grappling with ideas and exploring controversial topics as part of the learning process, presentation is an authentic demonstration of learning as part of a culminating public experience, which may or may not be assessed by the audience. The best presenters reflect deeply on what they think is worth saying. They make intentional choices about how to make their ideas clear and how they can use their physicality to highlight ideas. Like great orators throughout history, they do not shy away from sharing their own stories. Instead of using slides as a crutch, they use them to help their listeners think more deeply about their message. They consider how to communicate to build and strengthen a connection with the audience. They embody diversity by expressing who they are and what they care about.

Presentation as an Educational Tool

Our view of presentation falls well within the broader definition of *literacy* given by the National Council of Teachers of English (NCTE): "a tool for meaningful engagement with society." The NCTE also considers, however, how language and literacy have historically been tools for maintaining power, especially in imperialist and colonialist systems. These persistent inequities and power structures continue to shape how we view literacy. Although it is important to ensure that young people have access to formalized language tools, they must also have the chance to communicate the lives that they lead outside those structures. Emphasizing speaking and listening at least as much as reading and writing opens the door to focusing on the stories of young people, embracing all the languages they speak, and reinforcing the fact that diversity is beautiful. As Amber Peterson (2020), a member of the NCTE Standing Committee on Global Citizenship, states:

> Literacy is the way that we interact with the world around us, how we shape it and are shaped by it. It is how we communicate with others via reading and writing, but also by speaking, listening, and creating. It is how we articulate our experiences in the world and declare, "We Are Here!" (para. 11)

Educational standards for speaking and listening have focused primarily on the clarity of presentation content and delivery. Although clarity is incredibly important, it is only a first step to reaping the full benefits of presentation. In this chapter, we use the terms *speech* and *presentation* interchangeably. We specifically define *speech* as an umbrella term for multiple styles of public speaking, with a speaker delivering an oral set of remarks. We define *presentation* as a specific format of speech, often involving visual tools, with the purpose of informing, teaching, or persuading the audience through organized points and information.

The principles in this chapter apply to both individual and group presentations, with the added element of needing to decide on speaker roles in a group presentation. To adequately prepare young people to effectively present in their lives and postsecondary careers, they need to be not only clear, but also authentic, compelling, credible, polished, and connected to the audience. For many young people, it is already scary to stand in front of a roomful of peers and clearly articulate ideas; it is even scarier to take risks and make strong choices. It takes practice and preparation to be brave.

There are many benefits of presentation:

- Develops literacy and academic language
- Furthers organization skills and sequencing of ideas
- Builds research skills and the ability to communicate research and evidence
- Refines rhetoric and word choice
- Promotes empathy and reflection
- Supports synthesis and summary
- Develops delivery skills to captivate an audience and highlight ideas, interests, and passions

Equity Through Presentations

Intentional guidance is essential to disrupting patterns about who typically succeeds and enjoys giving presentations. Every classroom includes young people who enjoy speaking in front of a group of people or have already had experience performing publicly, such as through musical groups, leadership programs, or speech and debate teams. For those who have not had these opportunities or who prefer to listen rather than speak, presentations are often not the best way they express themselves or their knowledge. Rather than squashing the participation of those who get excited or stressing out those who feel nervous, guiding their preparation and practice advances an equitable classroom environment by addressing struggles before they have to present.

Getting Started

Assessments are the key starting point for unlocking a different kind of presentation because they can explicitly encourage diverse approaches and reframe the purpose of presentation. Rather than having learners summarize or repeat back their learning on a given topic (or even a topic of their choice), the purpose of presentations should be to raise new questions, share new and relevant information, take a stand, or present original ideas inspired by content learned. The following sections outline the steps for getting started with presentations in the classroom.

Design Rubrics to Encourage Diversity

To help learners make intentional choices about presentations, start by designing rubrics that require the presentations to be more than a summary of learning. In assignments and assessments, young people often see the instruction "Give a presentation." There may be logistical details about length, slide requirements, research to cover, and the deadline. Occasionally, learners are encouraged to express their opinions or answer a driving question or represent different points of view. Although rubrics often articulate requirements around content, they are rarely specific enough when it comes to articulating skills and dispositions. What is often missing are the presentation skills related to connecting with an audience, including (1) making choices about sequencing and oral delivery (or even what those choices are); (2) being able to adapt or stray from the script when the situation calls for it; and (3) showcasing their superpowers by taking risks, crafting a unique style, and being different.

Think of a presentation project you have previously assigned. What was the purpose? What did you want students to gain or demonstrate?

Would you say those goals were achieved by that format? Did you feel that anything was missing? How might including skill development have changed your students' presentations?

When designing rubrics that encourage diversity in presentation, focus on guiding questions or awarding credit related not only to the presentation's content and delivery but also to the authenticity, creativity, and risk-taking expressed by the speaker. Presentations should demonstrate how the learner is connected to the content, the meaning that has been made, and what has been learned. Adapting rubrics to different grade levels involves adjusting the overall number of focus areas and making language more approachable (see Figures 7.1, 7.2, and 7.3). Instead of points, you can have learners add stickers or use different colors to fill in the rubric as they make progress with each presentation. Cocreate rubrics with young people by having discussions about effective presentations, watching diverse examples, and giving them the opportunity to adjust the percentage/points that something is worth or adding guiding questions.

FIGURE 7.1

Rubric with Guiding Questions (Primary)

	My Reflection (stickers, colors, or writing in each row to illustrate self-assessment)	**My Teacher's Reflection** (stickers, colors, or writing in each row to illustrate teacher's assessment)	**My Friend's Reflection** (stickers, colors, or writing in each row to illustrate peer assessment)
What I said			
How I said it			
How I expressed myself			
How I connected to my audience			

FIGURE 7.2
Rubric with Guiding Questions (Secondary)

Point Scale
Still developing: 2–3 points
Meets standard: 4 points
Exceeds expectations: 5 points

Focus Area (with adjustable percentages)	Questions (To What Extent . . .) *Note: Questions shown here vary depending on the exact assignment, but serve as examples.*	Rating (2–5 points)
Content focus (10%)	• Did the content describe a compelling and significant issue using evidence? • Did the content cover an appropriate amount of material to support central ideas?	
Content effectiveness (25%)	• Was the content well-organized and clear? • Was the flow of the content compelling? • Were we swayed by the message?	
Delivery intentionality (10%)	• Were the delivery choices clear and apparent? • Were there distinct emotions? • Was there variation in volume, tone, and speed?	
Delivery effectiveness (25%)	• Were the delivery choices convincing and believable? • Were we drawn in by the overall performance? • Was the overall performance refined and polished? • Did delivery choices enhance the content?	
Authenticity (15%)	• Were we able to get a sense of the speaker as a person, in terms of their beliefs, background, or concerns? • Did the content clearly portray an element of the speaker's identity through creativity and strong choices? • Were we able to connect to the speaker's intent for their performance?	

FIGURE 7.2

Rubric with Guiding Questions (Secondary) *(continued)*

Point Scale
Still developing: 2–3 points
Meets standard: 4 points
Exceeds expectations: 5 points

Focus Area (with adjustable percentages)	Questions (To What Extent . . .) *Note: Questions shown here vary depending on the exact assignment, but serve as examples.*	Rating (2–5 points)
Risk taking and preparation (can also be replaced with teamwork) (15%)	• Did the speaker challenge their comfort zone? • Was it evident that the speaker went through multiple stages of preparation, practice, and feedback? • Did the speaker commit to their performance? If teamwork: • Did all group members contribute equally to the presentation? • Did the presentation clearly build on the ideas from each group member? • Was it evident that the team practiced and rehearsed together? • Was the presentation cohesive, and were individual presentations made better as a result of the team?	
Comments on notable elements		
Comments on areas to focus on next		

FIGURE 7.3

Rubric with Points (Secondary)

Point Scale
Emerging (4–5 points): Getting started, good effort
Developing (6–7 points): Some shining moments, but inconsistent
Meets (8–9 points): Solid skill base throughout the presentation
Exceeds (10 points): Memorable and impressive performance

Criteria	Element	Points
Content	Clarity	
	Reasoning	
	Use of facts/examples	
	Preparation	
Delivery	Voice (volume, modulation, diction, tone)	
	Physicality (gestures, eye contact, facial expressions)	
	Ability to hold audience's attention	
Authenticity	Personal passion	
	Use of storytelling and personal examples	
	Connection to the audience	
	Creativity bonus (extra 5 points)	
	TOTAL SCORE (out of 100 points)	

Comments:

Encourage Unconventional Approaches

Young people have more to offer than what the standard presentation requires, but deviating from the mold must be built into our teaching and the expectations we communicate to them. According to 16-year-old Elohiym Mudaavanha,

> What makes presentations boring is their lack of emotion. In schools, we are taught to be professional in order to prepare ourselves for the "real world", so that we can come across as mature and well-raised when we are in professional situations. I think that this is precisely what sets presentations back and makes them partially unbearable. As students, and as young minds, we should be able to put a full range of emotions into presentations, even if that compromises how professional it might seem. It also helps the students to be able to express themselves more clearly in the long run and will help their presentation become more meaningful.

Presentations will always come across as polished when they are driven by purposeful, specific, and intentional choices. As we have articulated throughout this book, young people need to know what specific choices are available to them and learn to question dominant norms. As 18-year-old Ella Bramwell shares,

> I think students need to be taught that presentations don't have to follow a certain formula. Presentations can be presented in thousands of different ways, and the best way to do them is whatever way is the most fun for the student.

Highlight Diverse Models

Young people should be exposed to diverse models of public speakers that represent and validate how they speak and what they want to speak about. Visions of success and professionalism that do not look or sound like them are disempowering. Presentations are an opportunity for young people to develop their identities as speakers and help them make choices in which they can take pride. As country singer Dolly Parton famously said, "Find out who you are and do it on purpose."

Telling young people that they have choices about how they want to present is not enough if they do not also have guidance about how to enact those choices and models for what they might look like. When asked how he prepares for speeches, Elohiym Mudaavanha said,

> What helps me the most is watching other presentations. Just by watching a professional presentation or one that is well received can get an idea of what my presentation is missing. By standing on the shoulders of those that came before me I can set myself up for success, anyone can.

Given how influential role models can be, make sure you show young people examples of presentations that reflect diverse situations, speakers, content, and approaches. Ask them what resonates with them and what specific choices the speaker made to showcase the message and captivate the audience. Create a folder or Pinterest board with examples of speakers (or assign this as a kick-off assignment or project) that reflect diversity in the following areas:

- Speaker's background (e.g., race, gender, and intersectional identity markers)
- Speaker's position (e.g., age, role, job title)
- Speaker's personal style (e.g., loud, quiet, humorous, reflective, light, forceful)
- Style of presentation (e.g., formal at a podium, more casual, multimedia)
- Situation and motivation for the presentation (where the speech took place and why—e.g., TED Talk, protest)

Be Mindful of Intersectionality

Presentations risk erasing or devaluing intersectionality when young people are required to speak one way and are unable to offer their own perspectives on a topic. In history classes in particular, asking learners to summarize historical events without the option of analyzing or offering different perspectives may perpetuate a version of history that does not resonate with the speaker. Even in math classes, presentations should offer a window into how young people are making sense of information, such as asking them to describe where they started in their understanding of a topic and how they evolved in that understanding.

Watching examples of presentations can also backfire if young people feel inspired by a model speaker but then become even more anxious because they feel like they are impossibly far from that standard. Conversations about role models should be starting points for highlighting presentation diversity, but the point is not to become that speaker. Ask listeners to identify the choices they made (e.g., changes of tone, hand movements, pauses, stories, examples used, data provided) and how effective they were at conveying their message, connecting with the audience, and leaving a lasting impression. Guiding young people through the process of making intentional choices helps bring them a sense of their own agency when it comes to presentations.

Anticipate Presentation Struggles

Similar to their experience with writing, young people can get stuck when they are coming up with ideas, figuring out what and how to research, deciding how to start and end a presentation, and elaborating further. There's the additional challenge of having to appear comfortable in front of a room of peers while being graded. Having an equitable chance for success requires guidance around brainstorming, structure, delivery, and emotional discomfort. All of this guidance also applies to group presentations. If learners do not receive this guidance, they may display the following common behaviors:

- Struggling to identify a topic and getting delayed or not completing the assignment
- Avoiding research or struggling with choosing search terms
- Spending too much time on slides and not enough time on what they will say (often resulting in reading off slides)
- Not organizing their thoughts, leading to stream-of-consciousness ideas

- Hiding behind the work of other group members and not speaking much
- Struggling with delivery, including difficulty being heard or understood or not capturing the attention of the audience
- Not practicing out loud, leading to stumbles and nerves
- Feeling panic or anxiety around the presentation

Guide Topic Choice and Central Idea

As they consider their topic choice, remind young speakers that they should focus on one central idea that anchors all the other examples, facts, and stories in their presentation. They should be able to summarize this idea out loud as one short "headline" sentence that they can remember without looking through their notes. The ability to do so can also ground them if they feel nervous.

When selecting their central idea, presenters should be driven by the need to find out what kinds of information and methods for displaying information will resonate most with their audience. Speaking is different from reading and writing because the listeners do not have the text of the speech in front of them. A speaker must think about helping people learn, listen, and remember new information, both about the topic and the perspective they are relating. Answering some guiding questions, such as those shown in Figure 7.4, can help learners to select topics or to narrow down their core idea.

Guide Content Structure and Flow

The crafting of presentation content should be driven by ideas, not slides. When preparing presentations, young people and adults alike too often immediately jump to making slides instead of creating outlines or talking points. Like written literacy, oral literacy can be developed by showing learners how to map the ideas and examples that stem from their central idea and clearly organize their thoughts before deciding where visuals are needed. Tactics used in writing are useful to speakers as well, such as brainstorming all the information they want to include and then bucketing or clustering the bits of information under larger themes.

FIGURE 7.4
Speaker Questions

Questions About Personal Motivations
- What topics or issues make me feel excited or eager to speak? Are there topics that make me lose track of time when I speak?
- How does my topic relate to my beliefs, background, and concerns? How will I communicate that personal connection?
- Is there something about my topic that will go unspoken if I don't say something?
- How do I feel most comfortable speaking and expressing my ideas?
- How will I challenge my comfort zone for the sake of communicating my ideas more effectively?

Questions About the Audience Experience
- What made me choose this particular content for this presentation?
- Why is it significant to my audience, and why should they care?
- What do they already think they know, and how can I challenge or build on that knowledge?
- What do they need to know now, and what can wait until later?
- What will help them listen and retain the most important information?

The sequence of points matters in speeches because the order and flow can help create a sense of buildup and momentum as well as help listeners remember the central idea. For example, beginning with a personal story can be a great way to connect the content to the audience. When it comes to the primary content, starting with the easiest concept that is closest to the audience's background knowledge can be a helpful way to ground people in the topic, before progressing to more complex material or unexpected twists in the presentation. Prompting young people to think about the destination of their presentation helps them consider the implications of their ideas and where they want to leave the audience, which should go beyond a simple summary on a final slide. Once they establish the sequence, speakers should decide roughly how long to spend on different points, based on how important they are to the central idea.

Once learners have determined the sequence of their presentation, they can decide which points need slides to help enhance understanding or to visualize a complex concept. Limiting the number of slides to those that truly add value to the presentation also helps speakers avoid reading off slides and treating every thought as worthy of a visual representation. On rubrics, slide requirements should account for a smaller percentage of the total grade, with expectations phrased through questions such as "Does the speaker use slides as a visual tool or illustration, without reading from them or letting them take over the presentation?"

Longer projects can feel overwhelming to some students, including English language learners and students with special needs. Whenever possible, create a graphic organizer to guide their brainstorming process, with components such as what they hope to cover in the speech, what they hope the audience learns, what background information they need to explain, any useful research they hope to find, and possible stories or examples that they may want to include, along with shorter deadlines they set for themselves for when to complete outlining, research, writing, and practicing. You can also introduce each part of the presentation separately to chunk the speech-writing process into more manageable pieces, having learners write one section and then practice saying it out loud before moving onto writing the rest.

Support Research Efforts

Research for their presentation is often where young people get stuck or rely on other group members to complete the task for them, especially if reading is a challenge. Avoid generic instructions such as "Do research for your presentation." Instead, offer the following more specific guidance:

1. Ask learners what parts of their outlines require more examples or detail.
2. Ask them to write down their search terms and need-to-know questions before they even open their browser and become overwhelmed by information overload.
3. Make sure they have a document open on their computer or a notepad where they can jot down notes or copy/paste good quotes

and evidence (under headers that have the author's name, citation, and link, so they can refer back to the source).

4. If they are stuck, ask them to picture the ideal reality in which they have all their relevant research completed. How would the presentation be different with that research? What kinds of evidence, background information, modern-day and historical examples, or stories would make a difference to the power of their presentation?

5. Remind them that it is OK if they cannot find much research. If the research process is not fruitful, learners can lose momentum and interest in their own ideas or feel like those ideas are not worth saying because no one reputable has ever written about them. In fact, learners should feel empowered to point out the lack of research on a topic that matters to them and raise awareness about the need for research and presentations like theirs.

6. Anticipate who might need to take a break before coming back to research.

7. Incorporate study-buddy activities that have learners doing research for one another to break up the process and to help them get "unstuck" by seeing their topic in a new light. Introduce the idea of "thought partnership," with young people sharing one another's thinking process. For example, during work time, you can ask the class if they need their thought partners and then have them take turns describing their progress, struggles, and questions, followed by suggestions from their partner.

Encourage Personal, Powerful Language

Presentation delivery is easily improved with language that evokes emotion. Using first-person "I" language and "feeling" words (e.g., "I am excited," "I was curious about") as well as writing in short sentences or repeating key phrases are suggestions that are sometimes discouraged in regular writing but particularly powerful when it comes to engaging listeners. The use of "I" language can bring a personal quality to speeches that are otherwise too distanced or dry. Short sentences can alleviate issues with speakers who talk too quickly because they force speakers to pause between statements. Putting writing aside and focusing on delivery can also be helpful when the class is more than halfway through the lead-up to the presentation and some are still stuck around research or deciding on their topic.

Guide Delivery Through Feedback

Regardless of the content they present, delivery is how most speakers are judged and also where they receive the least help. Telling a speaker to generally slow down or speak louder is not always actionable and may not actually align with the person's natural style or the goal for the speech. Young people who speak softly may have a naturally soft voice, and the feedback to "speak loudly" might cause them to shout or strain their voice, or might make them feel more anxious about sharing in a way that does not feel authentic. The issue is rarely solved with something as simple as a directive. Instead, feedback on oral delivery should be given in a way that recognizes the complexity of the issue and sharpens their natural style, helping them build confidence and giving them permission to be different. The solution should align with the underlying issue, which can vary. For instance, issues with volume can stem from the following situations:

- Lack of breath support, which requires deeper breathing and more core strength to carry the energy through to the end of a sentence
- Lack of enunciation, which can result in muffled words that seem too soft but actually just need more precision
- Stiff jaw or not opening the mouth enough, which can restrict the space needed for the voice to resonate
- Lack of commitment to ideas, which requires some rethinking about what the speaker really wants to say and crafting language to reflect that certainty
- Struggles with confidence about public speaking, which requires personal affirmations and setting personal routines to regain control

Because delivery issues stem from so many different sources, it is important to help young people practice new habits using smaller chunks (two or three lines) of text. Instead of telling them to fix something about their entire presentation delivery, help them have early success by applying feedback to something small.

It can be hard to offer this level of support for every learner in your class, but young people can coach each other on small chunks of text, especially when the speakers themselves identify specific areas to work on with a peer. There will never be enough time for you to personally coach speakers, but young people may get even more out of supporting one another and bonding over common anxieties or generating ideas together. Consider giving learners short checklists or two or three guiding questions to help them help each other. For example, learners in pairs can start with the phrase "This is what I have so far . . ." or practice delivering a specific section of their speech. The listener then has specific things to listen for and write down. A checklist might include points such as these:

- Offer two positive comments on what stood out to you about the speech.
- Offer one comment about how the speech could be clearer and easier to understand.
- Say one comment about how the language or voice could be more engaging or powerful.
- Offer one suggestion for what the speaker should do next.

It's always important for listeners to start their feedback with something they appreciated. Another possible feedback structure consists of what the listener liked, what the listener wants to hear more of, and one question or point of confusion. As a class warm-up, have learners practice with a model to clarify the process. (See the "Feedback" section later in this chapter for more on this topic.)

Guide Delivery to Highlight Ideas

Ultimately, the point of oral delivery should be to highlight the content. Whereas the content puts a young person's unique viewpoint into words, the delivery helps listeners notice and remember what made those words special. Content can be highlighted using the following elements:

- **Speed.** Varying how fast or slow the speaker talks can help listeners know when to pay particular attention. For background information or storytelling, speaking quickly can bring higher energy to keep the audience's attention. Slowing down at the end, during reflective moments, or during essential phrases can help the audience internalize ideas.

- **Pauses.** Beginning speakers of all ages are generally uncomfortable with silence, which leads them to weave in filler words, rush through thoughts, or trail off. It is important to help young people recognize that for audiences to truly understand an idea, speakers need to "let the dust settle" between ideas and pause for longer than they think they should (two to three seconds!) before moving on.

- **Physicality.** Eye contact, walking around, and gestures should be used intentionally when the content calls for it. Do not generally tell speakers to "use more gestures"; instead, tell them which lines could benefit from the additional emphasis of a gesture. Speakers should direct their eye contact to the same place as their hands, so that if they are gesturing toward a slide, they also look in that direction, or if they are gesturing toward a side of the room, they also look at audience members on that side of the room.

- **Tone and color.** Different words or ideas lend themselves to different vocal tones. Presenting a set of researched facts should sound different than telling a joke, relating a story, or delivering an argument. Although young people differ in natural style, they should think about how the tone might shift in each section of their presentation.

Like reading and writing, oral literacy requires explicitly teaching young people the technical strategies and vocabulary to make informed choices about how they present. Too often, young people walk away with one central takeaway about presentation: "Don't use filler words." Instead, they need guidance to know where their strengths are and where their perceived weaknesses originate. Do they say "um" because they are forgetting to pause, or do they say it intentionally because they want the presentation to feel more informal and down-to-earth? Do they say "um" because they are thinking about what to say next? If so, can they think about other ways to voice their uncertainty and describe how hard something is to say? Owning their natural speaking style is an important part of the process.

Longtime voiceover actor Thom Pinto designed the "Colors of Your Voice" method to describe the different vocal tones available to performers. See Resource 11 in The Practice Space's *Presentation Guide* at www.practice-space.org/presentation-guide for more information (Baines, 2020e). Among the 10 different colors, 5 are most relevant to public speakers:

- Red: Robust, enthusiastic, outgoing, excited, passionate
- Blue: Grounded, cool, intellectual, centered, calm, understated, subtle
- Green: Off-the-cuff, spontaneous, casual, fresh, breezy, conversational, noncommittal
- Orange: Warm, loving, kind, and encouraging
- Gray: Assertive, no-nonsense, tough, forceful, stark, businesslike

Color vocabulary offers a language for teaching learners how to think about tone variation and what tone of voice suits a speaker's message and style. One 9th grade English language arts teacher uses a color wheel for a weekly class routine. Students spin the wheel and practice speaking in the vocal tone of the selected color. At The Practice Space, we ask young people to "practice colors" by reading pieces of text. This activity is one of our most popular modules with young people, who say it helped them "feel in control" or "say things in ways I would never have said them before." When learners struggle with learning about tone and colors, we also show examples of speeches from famous speakers and ask them to identify the colors used, any color changes, and how they personally reacted to the speaker's tone. Getting the colors right is less important than being aware of the need to change tones to better reflect the message.

Warm-ups and delivery-skill drills are another low-risk, easy way for young people to loosen up and learn delivery techniques. Tongue twisters can be used to practice gestures and emphasis, especially when students are prompted to try saying them in different ways. "Confidence contests" are a fun warm-up, where one speaker starts with a statement of opinion, like "Blueberries are the best fruit because they are full of antioxidants." The next person says the same exact sentence but tries to say it even more confidently using their face, hands, tone, and volume. This repeats with the same sentence three to four times before starting with a new sentence. For more examples, see The Practice Space's Public Speaking Warm-Ups and Routines at www.practice-space.org/public-speaking -warm-ups-routines/.

Overall, it is advisable to weave in brief spurts of time to work on delivery throughout the lead-up to a presentation. You can have learners present out loud to partners, stand around the room practicing to walls, or even spend five minutes in the middle of class to take a "vocal break" and say their content out loud at the same time. In addition, reserve a minimum of one class period before a presentation to do a "dress rehearsal" in small groups solely focused on a checklist about oral delivery.

Supporting Mindset: The Curse of Starting to Speak Well

Unfortunately, being able to speak effectively can be a double-edged sword. The good news is that the more success individuals have with public speaking, the more capable they feel, the higher their self-esteem, and the more likely it is that they will want to speak again. Public speaking becomes an increasingly important part of their identity and a view of themselves that gets integrated into their *self-concept,* the overall idea of who they think they are. Over time, they raise their expectations for themselves, and others expect more from them whenever they speak. The bad news is that there is more for them to lose. The stakes are raised when they present or speak, and there is more fear of disappointing themselves and the people who expect more from them.

For many of our participants at The Practice Space, the experience of public speaking goes in waves: hard at the beginning, easier once they grasp the basic structure, and then harder again once they advance to leadership roles or when their peers start giving well-intentioned complimentary comments about how amazing they always are. Similarly, the clearer and more personally committed they feel about their ideas, the more personally motivated they feel to express them well. When they make mistakes or miss the mark, they feel the blow even more deeply.

The open-education resource *Communication in the Real World* (2016) outlines the process of self-concept and identity development as it pertains to oral communication and public speaking. The book cites "self-discrepancy theory" to illustrate the risk and "cognitive unease" that increases when speakers start to perform well and begin to say more important things. For young people who have had consistently positive experiences with presentations, it can be both motivating and upsetting when their later experiences do not measure up to their expectations. As stated in the book,

> When our actual self doesn't match up with our own ideals of self, we are not obtaining our own desires and hopes, which can lead to feelings of dejection including disappointment, dissatisfaction, and frustration. When our actual self doesn't match up with other people's ideals for us, we may not be obtaining [their] desires and hopes, which can lead to feelings of dejection including shame, embarrassment, and concern for losing the affection or approval of others.

Given the deeply social nature of presentations and public speaking, it is not only important for speakers to consider how they will connect with the audience; the audience has the burden to consider the speaker, including how they (the audience members) will help the speaker feel capable. The audience has an integral role to play in seeing speakers for who they are and who they are trying to be, and in helping them achieve their vision.

Teaching Learners How to Listen

In light of how complex and challenging presentations are for the speaker, it is unfortunate how little effort listeners put in. Generally speaking, people retain approximately 25 percent of the information they hear in presentations and are too often impatient or distracted (Nichols & Stevens, 2019). Distractions are heightened in schools with class sizes that are too large, in rooms that are too big, and during days that are too long. When faced with the prospect of giving presentations, many young people just want to get through the experience, and they are more focused on what they will say when it's their turn than on listening to what the current speaker is saying. They mirror the rest of the world, which is fraught with different forms of "bad listening." These include three that *Communication in the Real World* (2016) describes as follows:

- Narcissistic listening, when people listen to bring the topic back to themselves
- Aggressive listening, when people listen to attack someone else
- Distorted listening, when people incorrectly recall information, skew information to fit expectations or existing schema, or add material to embellish or change information

Practicing Active Listening

As listeners, young people need to develop listening habits that enable them to clear their brains and take in the voices of their peers, truly seeing and noticing them. In his 2011 TED Talk, "5 Ways to Listen Better," sound expert Julian Treasure outlines a few routines to build these habits, including spending three minutes in silence each day to reset and recalibrate. Other routines include the "mixer," an exercise that involves trying to count the individual sounds or "channels" you hear in a given space; and "savoring," an exercise that suggests enjoying the beauty in mundane sounds. He also emphasizes the rule of "RASA," a reminder for listeners to always *r*eceive, *a*ppreciate, *s*ummarize, and *a*sk.

Take community norms and expectations to the next level by reinforcing listening routines and practicing in-depth, active listening with your learners before engaging in presentations. Ask yourself these questions:

- What type of listening do you typically do? How does it change depending on context?

- What helps you better listen for connection and learning?
- What is your listening routine as a facilitator/educator?

Listening Without Feedback

When people listen, their default mode is often to judge; but some-times this should not be the intent. For certain stages in the drafting and practice processes, the point is for the speaker to just get something out there. Sharing personal stories is another moment when the point is to genuinely hear what someone else has to say without any action steps. Speakers who do not want feedback should have the chance to say they want people only to take in their words, without response. Protocols can be useful to help people resist the urge to critique or respond, such as listening dyads or constructivist listening, where structures are used to help speakers process emotions in pairs without interruption.

Although feedback can be important (and is discussed in detail in the next section), listeners do not have to judge to be useful to speakers. It is healing to know that someone has paid attention and noticed their work, especially for young people whose voices have been historically under-represented. For speakers who have been successful in the past, it can be a relief to know that sometimes they can just share their ideas in progress without having to meet past expectations.

Feedback

When it comes to presentations, specific feedback helps young people represent their best selves. For instance, it can be helpful for speakers to articulate a few goals for what they hope audience members will get from their presentation and how they hope to connect. Before giving feedback, get into the habit of asking reflection questions such as "How did that feel for you?" "What would you have done differently?" or "What went better than you thought?" so that the experience becomes about the learners and not about pleasing you or just getting it done.

When speakers have the space and skill to say something significant, they will have an increased sense of urgency about getting high-quality feedback. Feedback and audience reaction are appropriate when (1) the speaker feels like they have taken their performance as far as they can by themself; (2) the speaker is stuck and feels like they cannot move forward without help; and (3) the speaker is getting ready for an upcoming high-stakes performance, with no choice but to be evaluated.

Guiding the Feedback Process

Feedback must always be specific, kind, helpful, and actionable. It is important to avoid overwhelming the speaker with too many different comments, or giving feedback that is beyond what feels personally possible for the speaker (see Resource 11 at www.practice-space.org/coaching -guide/ in The Practice Space's *Coaching Guide* [Baines, 2020b]). A speaker who is still struggling to figure out a topic will find it difficult to follow through on the comment "speak with more passion." A speaker who has never worked on oral delivery will find it discouraging to hear "stop being so monotone."

During this feedback process, provide listeners with clear directions about where to focus their listening (e.g., content versus delivery) and how to respond (e.g., one thing they liked, an area of confusion, one action to take that would help the listener receive the content as intended). A checklist or rubric narrows down the possibilities for listeners so they don't give too many suggestions that overwhelm the speaker and helps focus on what will be assessed. Ask anyone giving feedback to separate comments about content from comments about delivery (see Resources 9 and 10 in The Practice Space's *Coaching Guide* [Baines, 2020b] for tips on coaching delivery and speech writing at www.practice-space.org/coaching-guide/).

Beyond giving guidance about kinds of appropriate feedback, it is important to remind learners that we should never strive to receive only positive comments or no comments at all. Ask young people to reflect on their own personal reactions to feedback and to share these reactions and their preferred methods for receiving feedback with their peers and with you. It is OK to ask for feedback yourself to model how you go about asking for help and articulating preferences. Consider the following questions:

- Do you currently offer opportunities for young people to provide you with feedback?
- In what ways do you demonstrate that you take their feedback seriously?

On the topic of how teachers approach feedback, 18-year-old Ella Bramwell has this to say:

> The biggest thing I wish teachers taught students about feedback is that it is okay to criticize something, it is okay to find something wrong with someone else's presentation, something you didn't like and it is okay to say that. I wish they taught students that when people give you feedback, it is not a criticism of you, it only applies to the presentation. I also wish teachers could receive feedback and listen to the feedback they are given.

When listeners offer feedback, it is good practice for speakers to ask for clarification or examples. They should record any oral feedback in writing and keep these comments in one place to revisit the next time they practice. Let speakers know they are free to disregard feedback or take a different direction, especially if they can explain why they choose to do so. Making clear decisions for themselves is not avoidance or laziness; it is an act of agency that can build confidence in their decisions about content and delivery.

The Importance of Specificity

The most common complaint young people have about feedback on their presentations is that both their peers and their teachers are too vague. As 16-year-old Elohiym Mudaavanha points out, "Feedback is necessary for growth, so don't be vague in your responses or too complicated to the point that you don't have time to spell out how well they did." Although people sometimes fear giving feedback because they do not want to discourage someone, shying away from specific comments does not make the speaker feel any better. Help young people use the rubrics offered earlier in this chapter to focus their feedback—for example, by saying, "I gave you high marks on content effectiveness because I found your content well-organized and clear, especially when you stated all your points at the start of the speech." Even younger learners can be expected to say, "I liked how they gave lots of detail." Elohiym continues:

> Just saying something along the lines of, "good job" doesn't always make a student feel like they did a good job and saying too much makes it hard for students to comprehend. I think the best course of action is to have a rubric that you can check off as you observe their presentation. Even with just three or four specific points, you can give them "tangible feedback" they can comprehend rather than intangible feedback like "good job".

Final Takeaways

Learners' confidence stems from self-awareness of their strengths and struggles and a growing sense of certainty about how a presentation will go whenever they have to speak. When presentations are driven by intentional choices about delivery and content, they are more accurate reflections of how young people think and feel. As young people are guided by more specific feedback and progressively feel more noticed and heard by their peers, they are better prepared to speak effectively when it is time to say something truly significant.

8

Self-Advocacy to Navigate Inequities

Today we are confronting some of the greatest challenges humans have ever faced, and we are in a long process of reconciling with the devastating harm caused by centuries of systemic oppression in the United States and around the globe. Developing creative solutions and shifting deeply held beliefs in an increasingly divided society will require a diversity of bold, visionary leaders who speak from the heart, reach for connection, and inspire change.

What transformations are then needed in our schools to ensure that every young person feels confident and prepared to speak up and lead? How can decision making by those in power be inclusive if a large majority of voices go unheard and the culture of white supremacy isn't questioned? Author and activist adrienne maree brown (2017) reminds us that "the more people who cocreate the future, the more people whose concerns will be addressed from the foundational level in this world" (p. 158). Without cultivating confident speakers who can speak in service of themselves and others, the world will continue to be a place where the needs of large portions of society are devalued and disregarded.

In this book, you have learned about Expression-Driven Teaching and various forms of oral expression to practice inside the classroom. We end with advocacy, which is how people engage their voice with the world and foster equity beyond the classroom walls. This chapter will address skills in both advocacy and self-advocacy because they are inextricably linked, and we will use the term *(self)advocacy* when referring to both. Just like reading and writing, (self)advocacy is an essential life skill that enables individuals to speak up for themselves and not only navigate the current inequitable systems they live in but also create a world where everyone thrives. It is a process of locating themselves in relation to others, seeing how their own needs and the needs of others are met or not met, and advocating for what they believe needs to change. In our experience, when people learn how to advocate for what they need and begin to find power in that, they inevitably want to use their voice to effect greater change—toward more equity, love, joy, and justice.

This chapter is structured around the experience of one young woman, Mistura Bankole, and what she shared in a recent interview about her own journey of reclaiming her voice, offering insights for the classroom along the way. We hope in her story you will see the incredible power of creating expression-driven learning experiences that have ripple effects far beyond the classroom walls.

Meet Mistura

At the time of this writing, Mistura Bankole was a 15-year-old who joined the Speech and Debate Club at her middle school in Vallejo, California, when her friend and classmate Elohiym Mudaavanha brought The Practice Space to their school to help start a debate team. In relating her story to us, Mistura shared what speaking up as a child was like in her household in Nigeria, where she spent the first six years of her life, and described the bullying and exclusion she faced throughout elementary school after immigrating to the United States, and the impact public speaking has had on her life. Since participating in speech and debate in middle school, she has gone on to participate in competitions, recorded a podcast, and helped start a speech and debate team at her high school.

When Mistura was a young child in Nigeria, there wasn't much room for her to be the outspoken little girl she already had become. Even attempting to contribute to casual everyday conversations brought feelings of judgment from the adults, as if she was a burden for "talking too much." She recalls, "It's as if they're putting you in a box where you can't really just explore that part of you. Like I said many times, having a voice and being outspoken, it's a beautiful thing. And if you try to squash that from a young age, it affects that child later on."

She remembers thinking about all the things she was expected not to do or say because she was a child:

> It was hard for me as a child to figure out who I can and can't be myself around. You'd have in this group though, that one adult or so who appreciates the kid that talks a lot. And for me, that was my aunt on my dad's side. I remember her just always sitting with me and having these long conversations . . . I knew I could be myself around this person. My parents are great, amazing people. I love them, of course. But they, at a young age—they do now—never gave me that room to be myself in that way.
>
> Then I moved here and I couldn't talk to that aunt as much. We talk on the phone every once in a while, but that was basically it. It was insane because from this outspoken girl who loved to speak her mind, I completely just . . . that was gone. And it was like that for quite some time, because coming here with the culture shock, it was real that's for sure. I faced a lot of bullying, and that put me again inside this box. I didn't have any person to help me step out of that box like I did back home. I didn't like talking because of my accent. I felt bad and ashamed of my accent. It's like, "The African kid cannot talk." That's what was going on in my head. Like, "The African kid does not get to talk, does not get to have a voice." It was really hard for me. I didn't know how to get out of that box myself.

The Role of Adult Allies

As infants, we instinctively cry to tell adults when we need food, sleep, or comfort. We are born with this instinctive survival skill to advocate for our needs, and yet this ability is conditioned out of most of us as we are told (both directly and indirectly) when and how it's appropriate to ask, what we are worthy of receiving, and in which ways we can respond when our needs are not met—which generally is expressed as "This is just the way life is." By age 4 or 5, most children have learned that getting their needs met is conditional, and so they often choose silence as the safest response.

This feeling of being "boxed in," as Mistura described, is not unique. As young people get boxed in by expectations, every label, stereotype, and oppressive system adds another layer to the enclosure they feel around them. Intersecting identities play a large role in the types of barriers they face in stepping outside that box. Yet, Mistura had her aunt. Ask yourself, *Who did I have? What adult made me feel like I could be myself, like I could express all the thoughts and ideas I had, and never made me feel like a burden for it? Who took me, my ideas, feelings, and curiosity seriously?*

Those adults play a critical role in young people's identity development and self-belief. Sometimes our efforts as educators can feel insignificant because our hearts are big and we want so much more for each young person we meet. However, this false perception discounts the impact of everyday small moments and relationships. Mistura reminds us of the significance of spaces where allies—or "coconspirators," to use Bettina Love's term (2019, p. 117)—help young people break through those boxes. Thinking back to Chapter 2, with its in-depth discussion of how to cultivate brave spaces, we can ask ourselves, *What do these spaces look, sound, and feel like? What is it that adult allies do or say, or their ways of being, that make young people feel like it's possible to express themselves? What are the small, meaningful moments that build someone's skills and confidence to (self)advocate?*

A Young Woman's Journey to (Self)Advocacy

Here is how Mistura describes her journey to (self)advocacy:

> At a very young age I was a victim of sexual violence. This was back in Nigeria. Thank goodness I'm out of that situation. It's definitely different [here] from what things are like back home. Here people uplift survivors who are able to tell their stories. People support survivors, which is something that I knew at such a young age was not going to happen back home.

I did my first Original Oratory speech [in 9th grade] and I was like, I'm going to write about this, because again, this is during quarantine late last year. Going back a little bit [to 8th grade], I did Oratorical Interpretation, [performing a version of] a TED Talk that I listened to a couple times. I love that TED Talk. I reached out to the person [Thordis Elva] who did the TED Talk who also wrote a book. I didn't expect her to respond because she's an influencer but she responds. I told her I want to use her piece for speech and debate. And she said, "Oh, have you read my book?" So she sends me a signed copy of her book, which I cherish. I would protect that book with my life. That was my first time ever opening up to someone about what happened to me. She was so supportive and she's a grown woman and has three kids. I was just like, whoa, you know? People can write about this.

So I decided to do just that for an Oratorical Interpretation piece. I wrote about it because Thordis Elva decided that she could either let this keep her down and let this be where she drew the line, like she was weak and that was that. But she was able to say, you know what, this is my form of power. So I decided that if she can do it, I can do it.

And I kept asking myself, are you going to do this? And I was like, yeah, I am, because I deserve it. I already knew writing was my form of taking back my power. So the first time I presented the speech to my speech and debate team, I was literally shaking so much, but they were so supportive and I'm like, this is too good to be true, but they were, and that was so beautiful to me.

I felt safe talking to Thordis Elva; I felt safe when my team was supporting me; I felt safe when Ms. Baines was checking up on me. Every single survivor deserves to feel this way. And even when I had an incident that happened recently, I still surprisingly felt safe thinking about the amount of people who are there for me. Even though I never really talked to them about it, I still felt safe. Like that feeling of imagining a hug from everyone that has ever been there for me. I feel safe.

What It Takes to Feel Safe

As Mistura reminds us, we have to feel safe in order to learn to (self) advocate. Establishing identity-safe classrooms where students can become increasingly brave as relationships are built is challenging but essential. By the time youth start middle school, peer pressure to conform to norms around coolness in order to belong, including not showing you care, plays a huge role in classroom learning. Unless that culture of feeling safe is intentionally built, peers can be less likely to voice encouragement and support of one another.

Youth need structure that fosters a different set of norms so they feel safe enough to show they care. Speakers need opportunities to build toward more vulnerability. Mistura didn't share her personal story to advocate for survivors of sexual violence in the first speech she gave. Having an opportunity to tell someone else's story helped her practice talking about the topic without having to reveal her own experience. For some, it feels safer to first advocate for others before learning to speak up for themselves. Often the journey toward (self)advocacy is slow. What established norms and opportunities for learning and experimenting with one's voice are helpful in this journey? Mistura's story about her own process offers some key takeaways about what makes that journey possible:

- Using listening approaches that affirm and uplift one another's voices and stories, starting when the stakes are low (see Resource 6 in The Practice Space's *Advocacy Guide* at www.practice-space.org /advocacy-guide/ [Baines, 2020a])
- Opportunities to perform someone else's story or published speech first (e.g., Oratorical Interpretation)
- Showing a range of public speaking models so that youth can see themselves and their experiences reflected, including examples of when (self)advocacy results in positive change and feeling empowered
- Offering and cocreating a range of (self)advocacy topics
- Providing time for students to research their topic and explore more models on their own
- Checking in with students individually along the way, especially when they open up about personal experiences

When establishing a safe environment for (self)advocacy, it is helpful to consider facilitation moves, including the following:

- Cocreating community agreements, including audience norms, speaker norms, and group norms, with do's and don'ts being especially helpful
- Posing different scenarios involving conflict and the need for advocacy, discussing what needs to happen for different voices to be heard
- Explicitly modeling how to respond productively when people want to agree or disagree with an idea, posting sentence-starters for reference
- Creating a culture of encouragement and validation of different perspectives, valuing diverse worldviews, and at times, agreeing to disagree

These types of opportunities helped Mistura face the fear of vulnerability, and she found the courage and confidence to speak. The fact that she received so much support from both peers and adults once she did face her fear meant she would keep sharing her story, and others were more likely to as well.

(Self)Advocacy as a Vulnerable Act

Even when they conclude that their message needs to be heard, some individuals are unable to position themselves as advocates. When asked to define (self)advocacy and what moments in her life represent (self) advocacy, Mistura reflected on the role vulnerability played in speaking up and why doing so is worth the risk:

> No matter how confident you are in that specific thing, or no matter how ready you feel, that fear is always going to be there. But here's the thing—that fear is probably the most amazing thing ever because of the feeling that comes when you overcome it. So when I think of

self-advocacy and advocacy, I think of vulnerability because you're breaking down all your walls for the greater good, because to be able to speak up about something, there's definitely in the back of your head, "I'm not the only one." There's obviously going to be someone out there who relates to what you're saying. Even though you don't see it, I think of it as an invisible army behind you, people who would support you and people who relate to whatever it is that you're deciding to speak out about. It's amazing because it's more than just a "me" thing.

I'm putting myself out there because there are other people who are going to understand it. And to do that, you have to break down all these walls. You have to put down all these barriers, and that's not always easy to do, but when you finally do it, it's incredible because you see yourself again in a whole new light. You're like, "I did that, and that's so amazing." *So it goes from vulnerability to empowerment*. And even if no one comes up to you and says, "Oh my goodness, you completely changed my life with what you just said," you know that feeling was there. I know I am not the only one.

Even amid the difficulty of making ourselves vulnerable by speaking up about something we deeply care about or need, being reminded that we're not alone can help us feel like it's worth the risk. Self-advocacy then goes from a "me thing" to an opportunity to help others as well as ourselves. Speakers can even imagine a specific person or group of people as their "invisible army," as Mistura describes it, supporting and resonating with whatever it is they've decided to say.

Situations Requiring (Self)Advocacy and Advocacy

So how do we build toward that amazing feeling of accomplishment and prepare youth to risk vulnerability? First, it's helpful to think about the situations that young people encounter now—and should be prepared for in the future—that require advocacy skills. People use (self)advocacy skills in a variety of contexts and situations, including within relationships (e.g., with a peer, parent, or teacher), when navigating institutions (e.g., in an IEP meeting), or speaking to a crowd, and there are different scaffolds, depending on the audience and purpose. Situations that require strong (self)advocacy skills include the following:

- Communicating expertise
  - Stating strengths and presenting evidence of expertise
  - Highlighting your side of the story
  - Networking and connecting with others
  - Suggesting specific action and concrete action steps
  - Recognizing skills yet to be developed

- Asking for help
  - Asking questions and communicating confusion
  - Expressing struggle
  - Stating specific desires and what you need and want

- Fighting injustice
  - Pushing back against injustice and wrongdoing
  - Educating people about diverse viewpoints and experiences
  - Proposing changes in existing structures (e.g., processes, laws, policies, norms)
  - Being an ally to others

- Expressing dreams

Being able to speak up in each of these situations is a highly valuable life skill, and practice is key. Use skits or role-plays with specific scenarios that young people are likely to encounter where they need to advocate for themselves. Provide prompts and sample responses to help them practice. This activity can also be extended to include advocating for others and having students create their own scenarios or responses.

Convey to learners that, even when people are able to advocate well for themselves, they don't always get what they need. The goal is a delicate dance: to cultivate agency in young people to navigate current inequitable systems and believe that a more equitable world is possible. At the same time, it is important to avoid the trap of perpetuating the myth that if people just work hard enough, they can do anything, which blames the individual if the goal is not attained. The "dance" requires exploring current power dynamics and interrupting them even as they play out in the classroom, while imagining what other possible futures could exist and the steps it would take to get there.

Why (Self)Advocacy Is Hard and Emotional

Just like many other things, (self)advocacy skills are taught in the context of particular students, experiences, and community. With a welcoming space already established, conditions should allow for conversations about existing inequities. Self-advocacy is about being able to speak up about a need; but to do that, people first must be willing to tell someone they need something. It doesn't feel good to need something, especially in the United States, where social norms encourage self-reliance over seeking community support. After identifying a variety of situations requiring (self)advocacy, ask students what makes it hard to advocate for one's needs, adding any from the following list if missed:

- Discomfort over "making it about me," "taking up space"
- Difficulty in expressing identity when sometimes you don't know yourself yet
- Fear of pushing back against sources of power
- Fear that your needs might not be taken seriously
- Need to feel sure of yourself and the difficulty of doing so if you feel like an outsider or an imposter or your voice isn't welcome
- Not feeling that your story and experiences are valuable
- Fear of the possibility that you or people you care about will be harmed by your speaking up

Building in time to unpack what makes (self)advocacy difficult, including cultural norms, frames any discomfort as part of a larger social context rather than an individual struggle. Due to its emotional nature, the sequencing of (self)advocacy activities is important. We suggest the following steps:

1. Start by discussing students' general observations, including naming any risks or dangers young people face when they speak up (e.g.,

the possibility of being arrested or even killed if seen as defiant by police).

2. Use journal writing to have students reflect on personal experiences, ones that boosted their confidence or made them feel silenced, and any role oppression or privilege played.

3. Have learners share stories about moments when they witnessed (self)advocacy in action, including its impact, if known.

4. Have them begin sharing their own stories in pairs or small groups. Some possible prompts include "Tell me about a time when you (a) told someone you wanted or needed something, (b) spoke up for yourself or someone else even though it felt hard, or (c) wish you had been able to speak up for yourself or someone else."

Part of this work is helping learners to see that they are not alone. As Mistura points out, the more people are able to advocate for what they need, the more likely those conditions will improve for everyone. However, it takes intentional scaffolding for young people to risk that vulnerability.

Making Room for Vulnerability

Although the use of equity sticks (popsicle sticks with students' names on them, used for calling on students at random) is often a go-to strategy to increase student participation, the experience can still feel paralyzing for young people who have yet to collect their thoughts or who worry about negative peer reactions. In regard to (self)advocacy, some people feel more comfortable advocating for their needs in close relationships but far more uncomfortable with strangers. Others are able to speak passionately about an issue they care about but not one they personally struggle with. Creating brave classroom spaces means making all learners and their unique voices feel welcome and valued. When Mistura was asked to describe what it would feel like to feel free in a classroom, she said this:

> I would feel comfortable. And by that I mean, not literally like pajamas comfortable, but I would feel comfortable enough to be myself in that environment. I get it that it is difficult for teachers to be able to build an environment that is suitable for every student, but if you do that little

part to make your students feel comfortable, it goes a long way. Not just academic-wise, but feeling comfortable and feeling safe goes hand in hand. If I'm able to feel as if this is an environment where I feel good about myself; this is an environment where I'm excited to learn; this is an environment where I know that I'm accepted and every part of me is accepted then yeah, I'm going to learn better. Yeah, I'm going to be a better student. Yeah, I'm going to pay more attention in class.

The power of creating spaces where young people will allow themselves to be vulnerable cannot be overstated. As Tema Okun (2021) states, "We are strongest when we are allowed to be vulnerable—with ourselves and each other. White supremacy culture does not allow for vulnerability. And that is a tragedy for us all" (para. 14).

Vulnerability looks different for each individual, and what feels like a risk to one person might not for another, so it's important not to have specific expectations in this area. Questionnaires, coupled with ongoing self-assessments, can help with understanding each person's initial comfort zone. Learners then can take an active role in reflecting on their growth as a speaker and (self)advocate. For teachers, these measures can also provide insight into areas that might need extra attention (e.g., building a more supportive listening culture), as evidenced in patterns of where learners still hold back. When teachers also model vulnerability through sharing who they are and where they come from, they are cultivating spaces that make it possible for youth to be vulnerable as well. When a supportive culture of belonging has been built, speakers have agency and choice about what they express, and as Mistura suggests, youth feel accepted for who they are. The power lies in the speakers' own hands to express what they feel most compelled to say, from seemingly insignificant commentary to important advocacy against an injustice they've faced.

Making Room for Agency

Equity is an environment, and creating equitable learning spaces means increasing youth agency in the classroom. Exerting agency is core to being human. And yet, young people are continuously stripped of this control over their learning, their time, and even their bodies, resulting in feelings of powerlessness over and over again.

As you reflect on your own classroom and lessons, here are some useful questions to consider:

- What parts of my lessons give students choice and creative freedom?
- What aspects of my tone, word choice, or content framing help students feel like this is a space where they can truly be themselves and be heard?
- What aspects of those elements could I shift to increase feelings of belonging?
- When are good moments in a particular lesson or unit to have students express what they need, want, or believe?
- As I diversify the forms of expression I teach, how will I include opportunities for learners to practice advocating for themselves and others?

Ultimately, we want learners to be able to make intentional choices about how they convey what they want to say. Developing that skill requires opportunities to try new approaches, to make choices that don't work, and to learn from the experience. Sometimes it means resisting the urge to correct young people's initial ideas, an urge that can convey a sense of superiority and doesn't lead to real learning. Mistura shares the lifelong effect of being able to speak up for oneself in a classroom:

> If you constantly make me feel as if because I'm a student I'm less than, I'm going to carry that attitude onward, like every authoritative figure is better than me because of whatever reason, which is completely untrue. We can't ignore the fact that even adults make mistakes and even adults don't always know what's best and we should be able to have students say, "You know what? I disagree with this and here is why."
>
> As a teenager, I understand that once you give students that kind of power, there's always a chance they're going to misuse it. But to be able to teach them that from a young age, that your voice does matter in this classroom, that sticks with them until they're older and they're

able to have moments where they do feel as if they need to speak up in a classroom. If you have first graders and explained to them, "If you don't agree with this, you can let me know. If you feel as if we should do something different, you can let me know." Obviously there's a good chance that they're not even going to use that power, but they understand that it's there. And when they're older that sticks with them. If I don't agree with something and if I'm not okay with something, I have the power to speak up.

And then you have students who at times need help with something and not even being able to ask for help because they're too scared because they don't want to put the teacher in this uncomfortable position where they have to go over things again, just because I don't understand something. I had a moment like that today in class where, even as outspoken as I am, I couldn't ask for help when I needed it because I thought the teacher's going to feel some type of way if I do ask for help. I realize it shouldn't be like this. I'm here to learn. I should feel as if I'm able to ask the questions I need to ask. But if that foundation is not set, where I feel as if I have a voice, then it's going to later on affect my education.

The following are tips Mistura shared for how teachers can create an environment where young people feel heard, valued, and increasingly confident about speaking:

Do—

- Give choices and room to express and be oneself.
- Let students know what specific skills they will gain, and discuss their lifelong use.
- Express the impact of feeling able to use your voice.
- Create a sense of community and belonging.
- Encourage speakers to ask questions.
- Acknowledge the challenge of learning to (self)advocate, and assure students that you will learn together.
- Let students know they can change their mind and making mistakes is expected.
- Be yourself and allow yourself to be vulnerable too.

- Show your students they matter to you.
- Strive to guide, not control.
- Remind speakers they're not alone—there will always be someone else who relates.
- Show varied models of speakers on diverse topics, including hearing different sides of an issue.
- Listen deeply; let what they have to say have an impact on you.
- Respond openly to their (anonymous) feedback and share any adjustments you will make because of it.
- Validate and uplift student questions, responses, and stories.

Don't—

- Box speakers in; let them make choices about their content, type of speech, and style.
- Assume what level of skill or knowledge students have.
- Try to control the outcome.
- Assume they always know how something you teach is applicable to life.
- Attempt to be someone you're not; authenticity is key.
- Project the impression that you are better or smarter than them because of age, life experience, or anything else.

Listening to What Youth Say

When we don't explicitly teach (self)advocacy skills, we often unknowingly invalidate young people's experiences and needs, thereby perpetuating systemic barriers to educational access and success. When learners have internalized messages that they aren't as smart or capable as others (e.g., "I'm just bad at this—everyone else is better than me") or that what they have to say is unimportant, those messages are often reinforced by not getting called on and by negative peer comments. Having learners identify areas of expertise, or the prior knowledge or skills they bring to a project, helps reposition them as experts (see Resource 7 in The Practice Space's *Advocacy Guide* [Baines, 2020a] at www.practice-space.org /advocacy-guide/). To take a stand on an issue, learners first must believe that they are deserving of something better, that what they have to say matters, and that it is, in fact, possible for conditions to change—a point that is not always addressed with youth.

Part of teaching these skills requires listening to young people, to their critiques and solutions, and opening yourself up to making changes. For learners to conclude that it is worth advocating for their needs, they must first see that doing so makes a difference. Just as developing speakers need moments of early success to build confidence in their voice, developing (self)advocates need to experience the impact their voice can have when someone truly listens. So be prepared and open to receiving feedback, and create opportunities to elicit student input on curriculum choices, what they want the classroom to be like, and lessons. Try integrating feedback into a classroom routine, such as through exit slips. If what they say never actually materializes or changes the conditions around them, however, feedback can do more harm than good by only reinforcing the belief that nothing can change. Listening is not always enough. Learners need to believe in the possibility that what they say can make a difference.

Freedom Dreaming: The Need for Imagination

Establishing a foundation for vulnerability and agency opens up opportunities for dreaming and healing. Bettina Love (2019) reminds educators that imagination informs what is possible, and the radical changes needed in our education system, in our world, start there. She speaks to the significance of such imagining:

> My entire life is possible because dark folx freedom-dreamed. These dreams were filled with joy, resistance, love, and an unwavering imagining of what is possible when dark folx matter and live to thrive rather than survive. These freedom dreams and the places that helped them move into reality are important markers of what is possible. (p. 93)

When Mistura thinks about the future, she imagines creating a business that increases access to halal products for Muslims. She also knows she will continue to use her voice to end sexual violence, and she hopes to help address its root causes. As she elaborates,

> In terms of sexual assault, I'm not letting that one go. It's still something that I want to be an advocate for. You know how you'd have people at school assemblies come give a speech about a specific thing? That's what I think of, where I'm going to go: me on a stage with a bunch of high schools and explaining to them the importance of why we should care about this and what it means to be a survivor and having an organization set on being there for these survivors. That's what I see myself doing.
>
> Without those roadblocks, the ideal world would be to use that time to focus on more important things. So if we didn't have to constantly worry about sexual assault survivors being believed, then we'd be able to focus on, how do we stop these perpetrators? Or how do we remove that mindset where it's okay to hurt people this way?
>
> And when we're able to eliminate the parts holding many people back, or the part that makes it difficult to push forward, that's when I believe that real change starts to happen. If you're able to push things to the next level. So the hardships are out of the way, now what comes next? To be able to get to a point where we understand what needs to be changed and we're changing it. How do we make sure this change stays in place? That's the biggest thing for me. It's just a matter of figuring out, where do we start?
>
> I realize now that if I didn't have the foundation that I have now, I wouldn't be able to think that far. But I see myself in the future being able to build on what I already have here for me, which is the foundation of good public speaking skills, this foundation of this support system. That's a big one for me—the support system that I have here, the connections that I have through [The Practice Space] and being able to build on that and take that into the real world and apply that into what I do in the future.

Imagining freedom starts with certain kinds of knowing: knowing that realities exist outside your own, knowing the ways people fought for future generations to have freedom that they would never themselves experience, knowing that innovation and change require questioning what's accepted as fact, and knowing unequivocally that you and all human beings matter enough to make what you've imagined a reality.

Bettina Love points to what education philosopher Maxine Greene once said:

> To commit to imagining is to commit to looking beyond the given, beyond what appears to be unchangeable. It is a way of warding off the apathy and the feelings of futility that are the greatest obstacles to any sort of learning and, surely, to education for freedom. . . . We need imagination. (Greene, 2009, cited in Love, 2019, p. 102)

Love continues: "These freedom dreams drive out apathy, and the quest for freedom becomes an internal desire necessary to preserve humanity" (p. 102). Real change is made possible by young people like Mistura when we equip them to tear down the barriers they face and build an inclusive, equitable world in its place.

(Self)Advocacy and The Power to Heal

Learning to advocate on behalf of what you or others need is a vulnerable act not to be rushed. It is not a box to be checked off a list. As Mistura's story has revealed, it is an ongoing journey made up of small moments and lifelong impacts. This chapter has shared specific strategies that aid in the process, such as creating necessary classroom conditions, and having students engage in activities such as role-plays or mapping their expertise. But more than anything, (self)advocacy is the expression of confident speakers who are determined to make a change and believe they matter enough to do so. It is about reclaiming your voice, and as Mistura shares, it has the power to heal:

> I chose the topic [of sexual violence] because of a personal experience for me, and the quarantine was a really big time for me to find myself because I wasn't around as many people obviously, and I was in my own head a lot. I realized now that I have this thing, which is a voice. It's so powerful. I see myself using speech and debate as a way

to convey the things that I stuffed down inside. I connect it back to my source of power, which is my voice.

And even though it's not the norm, and everyone deals with stuff differently, obviously, I found that being able to take the things that I would bury down or the things that I push aside and turning them into words helps me, because I'm able to sit down with my feelings more, like I got to do over quarantine, sit down with myself, sit down with the parts of me that I hide away. My words are my way of doing that. Public speaking is my way of doing that. Because again, I'm getting to use this thing that I took for granted for a long time, which is my voice. For me, it's more than just a speech—it's my way of dealing with it all because these are moments in which I felt weak, you know, and weakness is something that I always just keep in mind. I felt powerless. But then I have this speech that I was able to write down on paper, and it's less about winning competitions for me, it's more like, you did that! You're not weak, you're powerful. I realized that after I've done this speech and the competition is over, forget the trophy, I did that. And that's what plays into all the decisions and topics that I choose. That's my form of power.

Final Takeaways

There are moments in life when an experience can feel like it will silence you forever. If we take one thing from Mistura's story, let it be that education in public speaking involves far more than knowing how to give a presentation. Building a new way forward, one that serves the diversity of human needs in this world, is possible. Gaining the confidence to express who you are and what you care about has the power to heal, to find strength in your unique voice and feel excited to share it with the world. This form of community healing, not just for speakers but for those who have the privilege of hearing their stories, is a direct challenge to the oppressive systems that divide us. Instead, in their place is the humanity that connects us.

Final Word

Comfort Zone

My comfort zone is a familiar place
All the things I know live here in harmony
There are lots of places to sit
And keep track of things
like rules and fears and failures
No one judges me here . . .

When you step outside a comfort zone
the zone grows but the comfort shrinks
One becomes exposed to new elements
It's like being trapped in a barrel
floating towards that part of the river
that becomes a steep waterfall
I can see it on the horizon
I know when it is coming
Yet I brace myself for the fall

There is no safe spot to run back to
It's like playing hide and seek
with your demons and destiny
But in this game, you are always it
there is no hiding, there is only seeking

Whatever you do out here
can lead to embarrassment or triumph
The territory outside our comfort zone is
equal parts dread and possibility
No wonder we don't like leaving it

—Diana Medina

Public speaking happens all the time. It takes place any time we express our ideas aloud to someone else, hoping they will listen. It takes place in a crowd, during team collaboration, during classroom instruction, and in storytelling with friends. It is how we connect, learn, and get work done. It is how we share our identities and get inspired. Public speaking is how we live.

The importance of public speaking is what makes it so scary and dangerous. You are told to "be yourself," but dominant societal standards for what a speaker is supposed to look like and sound like fit only a privileged few. In our public speaking classes at The Practice Space, we hear women, girls, and youth of color make statements such as "I don't want to get so emotional," "I want to use bigger words so I'll be respected," and "I just want to sound like everyone else." When who you are isn't valued, it makes sense that you will want to erase yourself: not being valued is what you have been taught to expect.

Pursue Freedom of Voice

It is time to teach toward a new reality, and public speaking education should help young people feel capable, cared for, and free. Freedom comes from knowing what to do, understanding your own thoughts and feelings, having the chance to be creative and break the rules, and knowing that your full self will be celebrated because there is space to be you. For a young person, freedom of voice means being able to do the following:

- Define yourself without being hindered by the weight of societal stereotypes

- Feel and express emotions, knowing you are safe enough to be vulnerable
- Share what is important to you, even if it is different
- Know that people will genuinely listen to you and take you seriously
- Make choices about what you want to say and how
- Build genuine connections with people around you
- Enjoy being weird, awkward, and different
- Take risks and disagree productively to drive everyone's learning
- Believe you are getting better at expressing yourself
- Be so immersed in what you are preparing/performing that everything else fades away
- Laugh, be joyful, and have fun sharing your voice with the world

If these qualities are the "north star" of expressive experiences, a first step is to look for indicators that signal freedom of voice. Although every young person is different (and age and life experiences certainly play a role), you should feel satisfied when you see young people jumping into an activity because they feel comfortable enough to speak. It is a point of pride when they tell stories from their lives, no matter how seemingly inconsequential. Even when they struggle, we should take it as a good sign when they stick with their preparation, advocate for their needs, or ask for feedback because they care deeply about what they are preparing to say. The communication of real, genuine emotion means that someone's voice is a little bit more free.

Embrace the Mess

Creating spaces that cultivate freedom of voice often directly conflicts with the image of a compliant, quiet classroom where everyone consistently makes progress toward standards. During a coaching session, Tania, a 3rd grade teacher in our Youth Voice Advocates program, expressed how she felt bad when she saw another teacher doing math across the hall because she suddenly felt her storytelling activity wasn't rigorous enough. She found comfort in realizing how storytelling was not only valuable in itself, but also made her students noticeably happier, engaged, and ready for learning. Her story is a reminder that freedom of voice is impossible in a system where student engagement and happiness make a teacher feel bad.

Even as authors of this book, we still struggle to embrace the mess. For Caitlin Healy, teaching always involved the pressure to make student voice look a certain way, with a tidy progression of skills leading up to a preconceived notion of "good speaking" that didn't always leave enough room for authentic expression. She knew her vision was influenced by white, male-dominant public speaking norms, but it was hard not to feel like something was wrong when classroom engagement became messier than the "ideal." After more than 20 years of teaching public speakers, AnnMarie Baines still feels this way, especially on days when the classroom gets loud and unruly, or when learners don't seem to be progressing. Even knowing it takes a long time for speakers to develop communication skills is cold comfort on days when "youth voice" sounds more like chaos.

What is comforting are the memories of what youth voice looks like over time. A single day in class might be messy, but sustaining this work can coax out leadership, creativity, and inspiration in places where we may not have initially expected to find those qualities. The process shouldn't be effortless if we believe that youth are worth the effort. In one of our highest-need schools, the noisiest classroom has resulted in a powerful example of mentorship, with graduates coming back to volunteer in the classroom. Young people who previously required so much guidance are now guides themselves, and the reluctant scribbles on discarded notebook pages have transformed into speeches that inspire people to listen. The effort takes time, but it doesn't take forever. As activist bell hooks (1994) puts it best, "I had to surrender my need for immediate affirmation of successful teaching (even though some reward is immediate) and accept that students may not appreciate the value of a certain standpoint or process straightaway" (p. 42).

It is hard to appreciate struggle in a system that frames success as easy and effortless. This is the same system that treats first-generation leaders as imposters, children of color as troublemakers, mental health challenges as productivity issues, and emotion as weak. For Diana Medina, being a first-generation student meant she often heard people say, "We are giving you this opportunity." She regularly felt like she needed to keep important parts of her identity hidden away and that she was "too emotional" when it came to her work with Latino families. Years later, Diana reflects, "It *is* emotional when I am working with someone who looks like my mother." For Diana and so many young people, we owe it to them to create experiences that encourage the expression of emotion, rather than silence it.

Foster Identity Out Loud

The ultimate goal of Expression-Driven Teaching is for young people to express their identities and cares out loud. Public speaking has an important role to play in creating the conditions for listening and confidence and cultivating the ability to open a window into personal experience. In one of our classes focused on giving issue speeches about the most significant problems in our society, a 10-year-old speaker wanted to give a speech listing the qualities of 100 "underrated" dogs, one by one in great detail. It was tempting to get him to focus on something more "important," but even that urge made us pause. What made his choice less important? What made our ideas better? Wouldn't he still learn to become a better speaker, especially if he was able to speak in his own way? To his credit, he adamantly refused to budge about his topic, reminding us of what our role should truly be: to help young people make informed decisions about what is important to them and be able to express themselves in the most effective way possible. For us, our job was to help him create the best underrated-dog speech possible.

Start with Listening

When young people start speaking up for themselves effectively, we understand more about what they really think and feel. As bell hooks (1994) reminds us, "The exciting aspect of creating a classroom community where there is respect for individual voices is that there is infinitely more feedback because students do feel free to talk and talk back. And yes, often this feedback is critical" (p. 42). Student feedback requires us to unlearn the urge for constant control. Strong, active listening starts when we don't think we have all the answers and we truly need to listen to young people to discover their truths. Doing so takes incredible patience, a genuine interest in people, and a reminder to ourselves that we love and care about young people, especially on tough days.

As listeners, we can be the facilitators that young people need to embrace and navigate difference. When you have a unique perspective, it is even more important to say it clearly. When your voice has been under-represented, the stakes are higher to express it effectively. When no one else shares your experience, it is highly likely that the audience will get confused or even defensive and hostile. Preparing young people for these situations means equipping them with the confidence to believe that their voice matters and they will know what to do.

Create a Space to Practice

The work involved in developing youth voice begins with practice. Throughout this book, we have emphasized the importance of building relationships and a sense of safety as the foundation for youth voice, especially for young people who have been historically underrepresented or oppressed. We have explored the power of different modalities to offer new entry points for equitable participation or to explore new reasons why youth might speak. We have shared young people's perspectives that highlight the emotional journey involved in becoming intentional speakers who can express their identity and navigate barriers without internalizing them. For both young people and educators alike, this is complex work and much harder than teaching people to master mimicry. It is easy to get discouraged doing such developmental work—work that is never done.

To sustain this work, we all need opportunities to practice in front of audiences that are friendly and intimidating, interested and distracted; in settings that range from large crowds of strangers to intimate gatherings with family and friends. Public speaking wouldn't be the same without the "public," and these performance milestones break up the journey and give us all something to work toward. Young people need these opportunities to give shape to their goals, and educators need these moments to witness youth achievement and feel proud of the part they played. We seek hope in the tiny universes we create so voices can be heard. These powerful memories give us a chance to see young people for the incredible human beings they are, and for them (and us) to know it was all worth it.

Acknowledgments

Youth inspire and inform our work every day. Their stories and experiences offer us a valuable window into the emotional work of growing up and becoming whole in a deeply inequitable world. As they navigate these inequities, we are constantly struck by how hopeful and thoughtful they are on their quest for freedom of expression and self.

We are incredibly grateful to the youth who wrote pieces for this book, including the following: poems from Sheila Mckinney; quotes from Ava Acosta, Vidita Bhatt, Ella Bramwell, Jacob Klein, and Elohiym Mudaavanha; in-depth interview with Mistura Bankole; and stories from Everett Aishiteru, Elizabeth Duarte, Will Flowers, Cole Guimaraes, Eva Pelayo, and Genevieve Simmons. We are honored to have the support of our Junior Board of Directors at The Practice Space, whose beautiful words begin this book. A huge thanks to Mistura Bankole, Mariana Castro, Amber Crenna-Armstrong, Will Flowers, Lindsey Lam, Elohiym Mudaavanha, Mercy Niyi-Awolesi, Michael Schoonover, and Gloria Zearett. And thank you to those who preferred not to publish their names.

This book is dedicated to all educators and coaches who work tirelessly to guide and strengthen the voices of young people. In particular, we would like to thank those who made it possible for us to write this book, by reviewing our writing and shaping our ideas. Thank you to Jorie McDonald, Leona Kwon, Joel Jacobs, Mary Ann Lafosse, Michele Lamons-Raiford, Bob Litan, and Charles Peck.

Writing this book was truly a labor of love and passion, which would not have happened without The Practice Space community. Thank you to Angela DeBarger and the William & Flora Hewlett Foundation for funding this work and giving us the time we needed to write about youth voice and produce open educational resources to support the implementation of Expression-Driven Teaching. The Practice Space staff kept us strong and capable of finishing this manuscript, and we owe a great deal to Margot Aishiteru, Jumanah Alsawaf, Jim Bruce, Caroline Clarke, Amber Crenna-Armstrong, Morgan Cutter, Maribel Lopez, Maddy Shenfield, and Ja'Mes Williams. And thank you, as always, to The Practice Space Board of Directors for helping our nonprofit grow and elevate underrepresented voices: Paul Baines, Ione Bell, Lorna Contreras-Townsend, Todd Groves, Arthur Guimaraes, Johnny Lin, Elaine Lin-Hering, Maria Resendiz, and Sylvia Sudat. We extend our deepest appreciation to Stephanie Bize, Allison Scott, Liz Wegner, and the entire team at ASCD.

Our work has deep roots, and we are constantly learning from the voices of Black feminists like Bettina Love, Audre Lorde, and bell hooks and the liberatory education work of intellectual leaders like Paulo Freire. Our work also has personal roots, and each of us would personally like to appreciate our loved ones and trusted advisors who keep us grounded.

- From Caitlin Healy: I would like to thank Jake Nicol, my partner who took on more childcare and emotionally supported me so I could take the time I needed to write. Thank you to my son, Oscar, who withstood me dedicating so much time to something other than him when he doesn't yet grasp its significance. I am grateful to Tamar Sberlo, Sara Tiras, and Jessica Chen for sharing classroom experiences and having critical conversations that greatly supported the research and writing process. And finally, thank you to all of my teacher mentors, especially Melanie Blagburn, Alex Harp, Sonal Patel, and Gaia Pine for your guidance on how to support all learners, and that authentic expression comes in many forms.

- From Diana Medina: I would like to thank my parents, Jose and Natalia Medina, who gave me the best of both of them and struggled so that I could thrive. To my big, hilarious Mexican family—gracias for giving me endless material for my stories and poems. Thank you to the passionate poets I interviewed for this book (Alejandra, Ike, Kellz, Len, Sarah, and Cloudy) whose love of poetry continues to inspire my own and whose insights are sprinkled on these pages. Thank you to my friend and mentor Lisa Cantrell, executive director of Capital Storytelling, whose support, community, and guidance helped me discover and fuel my storytelling practice. To my big sister Velia Casillas: thank you for sharing your teaching expertise with me every time I call to ask for it and for your commitment to empowering me and the young people you teach. I couldn't do this work without Kika, my beloved fur baby, who sat on my lap or by my side offering cuddles and comfort while I wrote and edited these pages.
- From AnnMarie Baines: Writing this kind of book takes a lot of emotion and love. Thank you to everyone who helped make my dream of starting The Practice Space into a reality! I owe a great deal to the world of speech and debate, especially the late Catherine and Sanford Berman and my friend, Audrey McIntyre, who started me on this journey of building confidence in my voice. My heartfelt gratitude goes out to my friends who supported me, in particular, Sylvia Sudat, Shelli Bueno, and Sayaka and Nate Torra. I couldn't have done it without the love of my family, Adela Darrow and Aurora Darrow, and my late father, Steven Darrow, who always believed in me. And to my husband, Paul Baines: this book is possible because you love me, keep me strong, make me laugh, and encourage me to be me.

This book is a part of us, and we hope it helps many more young people to express the joy they have within.

Glossary

Debate: structured, civil discussion, which involves at least two sides to an issue, focuses on substance, features time limits for each side, and compels speakers to persuade an audience about how to make informed choices, incorporate new information, and identify ways to reach consensus.

Educational equity: an environment that (1) reduces the predictability of success and failure, (2) disrupts inequitable power dynamics and promotes shared power, (3) maximizes opportunity to showcase strengths and interests, and (4) minimizes the impact of oppression.

Expression: an all-encompassing range of modalities for youth voice that go beyond the classic speech or presentation format and include such forms as storytelling, podcasting, interviewing, conversation, and poetry.

Expression-Driven Teaching: a facilitation method for creating brave classroom spaces to speak and listen and to shift mindsets around which voices are valued and why. It guides how to develop the communication skills and inclusive environment necessary to cultivate youth voice and joy, while also creating opportunities to learn from the voices of young people.

Identity-safe classrooms: environments where student experiences and backgrounds are valued and students believe that their social identity is an asset, rather than a barrier to success in the classroom, and that they are welcomed, supported, and valued.

Intersectionality: an analytical framework for understanding how aspects of a person's social and political identities combine to shape experiences with discrimination and privilege.

Oral literacy: the explicit education and development of speaking and listening skills to construct and communicate meaning through voice.

Presentation: a specific format of speech, often involving visual tools, with the purpose of informing, teaching, or persuading the audience through organized points and information.

Public speaking: any form of oral speaking or verbal expression that involves communicating with another.

(Self)advocacy: the inextricably linked skills of self-advocacy and advocacy, used to speak up for one's rights, desires, and needs while navigating current inequities, toward more self-belief and love, vulnerability, healing, collective care, and self-determination, in order to create a world where everyone thrives.

Speech: an umbrella term for multiple styles of public speaking, in which a speaker is delivering an oral set of remarks.

Storytelling: a narrative tool to express human experiences by using detailed description to entertain or to provide a window into someone's journey.

Voice: the communication of a person's identity, expressed through verbal or nonverbal interaction with others, even when someone does not have the ability to physically speak.

Youth voice: the authentic communication of youth identity, with the capacity to be developed over time to effectively express opinions, cares, feelings, needs, and experiences.

References

Baines, A. M. D. (2014). *(Un)learning disability: Recognizing and changing restrictive views of student ability*. Teachers College Press.

Baines, A. M. D. (2020a). *Advocacy guide*. The Practice Space. https://www.practice-space.org/advocacy-guide/

Baines, A. M. D. (2020b). *Coaching guide*. The Practice Space. https://www.practice-space.org/coaching-guide/

Baines, A. M. D. (2020c). *Confidence-building guide*. The Practice Space. https://www.practice-space.org/coaching-guide/

Baines, A. M. D. (2020d). *Debate guide*. The Practice Space. https://www.practice-space.org/debate-guide/

Baines, A. M. D. (2020e). *Presentation guide*. The Practice Space. https://www.practice-space.org/presentation-guide/

Baines, A. M. D. (2020f). *Storytelling guide*. The Practice Space. https://www.practice-space.org/storytelling-guide/

Bauminger, N., Finzi-Dottan, R., Chason, S., & Har-Even, D. (2008). Intimacy in adolescent friendship: The roles of attachment, coherence, and self-disclosure. *Journal of Social and Personal Relationships, 25*(3), 409–428.

brown, a. m. (2017). *Emergent strategy: Shaping change, changing worlds*. AK Press.

CAST. (n.d.). Until learning has no limits. https://www.cast.org/

Castillo, M. H. (2020). *Children of the land: A memoir*. HarperCollins.

Chardin, M., & Novak, K. (2021). *Equity by design: Delivering on the power and promise of UDL*. Corwin.

Chávez, V. (2005). Silence speaks: The language of internalized oppression and privilege in community based research. *Metropolitan Universities, 16*(1), 9–25.

Cohn-Vargas, B., Kahn, A. C., & Epstein, A. (2021). *Identity safe classrooms, grades 6–12: Pathways to belonging and learning*. Corwin.

Collins, B. (2005). Poems on the page, poems in the air. In M. Eleveld (Ed.), *The spoken word revolution: Slam, hip hop & the poetry of a new generation* (p. 3). Sourcebooks MediaFusion.

Communication in the real world. (2016). [Author and publisher names removed at request of original publisher; adapted by the University of Minnesota Libraries Publishing]. https://open.lib.umn.edu/communication/

Cox, T. (Host). (2011, November 25). *Collecting oral histories of Jim Crow.* NPR. https://www.npr.org/2011/11/25/142704485/-collecting-oral-histories-of-jim-crow

Crenshaw, K. (1989). Demarginalizing the intersection of race and sex: A Black feminist critique of antidiscrimation doctrine, feminist theory, and antiracist politics. *The University of Chicago Legal Forum 140,* 39–167.

CRRJ Archive. (n.d.). Killing of Della McDuffie in Alabama in 1953. https://crrjarchive.org/incidents/323

David, E. J. R., & Derthick, A. O. (2018). *The psychology of oppression.* Springer.

Daza, E. J. (2020, September 25). How a "secret Asian man" embraced anti-racism. *LAist.* https://laist.com/news/race-in-la-how-a-secret-asian-man-embraced-anti-racism

Digh, P. (n.d.). A quote from *Four-Word Self-Help.* Goodreads. https://www.goodreads.com/quotes/825629-the-shortest-distance-between-two-people-is-a-story

Du Bois, W. E. B. (1903). *The souls of Black folk.* A. C. McClurg.

Eisner, M., & Escaja, T. (Eds.). (2020). *Resistencia: Poems of protest and revolution.* Tin House.

Enfield, N. J. (2017). *How we talk: The inner workings of conversation.* Basic Books.

Field, S. (2021, March 11). 4 equity levers in project based learning. *PBLWorks.* https://www.pblworks.org/blog/4-equity-levers-project-based-learning

González, N., Moll, L. C., & Amanti, C. (Eds.). (2009). *Funds of knowledge: Theorizing practices in households, communities, and classrooms.* Routledge.

Gordon, A. (2019). The linguistic dominance of white, western, English and how to recognize and disrupt it: A conversation with Dr. Samy Alim. *Pittsburgh City Paper.* https://www.pghcitypaper.com/pittsburgh/the-linguistic-dominance-of-white-western-english-and-how-to-recognize-and-disrupt-it/Content?oid=14230061

Gorman, A. (2021, January 20). Amanda Gorman reads inauguration poem, "The hill we climb" [Video]. YouTube. https://www.youtube.com/watch?v=LZO55ilIiN4

Gorman, A. (2021, January 28). Amanda Gorman—"The hill we climb" and activism through poetry [Video]. *The Daily Social Distancing Show.* https://www.youtube.com/watch?v=IRGO5g1rqTw&t=187s

Greene, M. (2009, Summer). Coda: The slow fuse of change—Obama, the schools, imagination, and convergence. *Harvard Educational Review, 79*(2). https://www.hepg.org/her-home/issues/harvard-educational-review-volume-79-issue-2/herarticle/obama,-the-schools,-imagination,-and-convergence_7

Growney, J. (n.d.). Intersections—Poetry with mathematics. https://poetrywithmathematics.blogspot.com/

Hall, E. D. (2018, May 11). Why we judge others. *Psychology Today.* https://www.psychologytoday.com/us/blog/conscious-communication/201805/why-we-judge-others

Heinrichs, J. (2007). *Thank you for arguing: What Aristotle, Lincoln, and Homer Simpson can teach us about the art of persuasion* (1st ed.). Three Rivers Press.

hooks, b. (1994). *Teaching to transgress: Education as the practice of freedom.* Routledge.

Illich, I. (1971). *Deschooling society.* Harper & Row.

LeBron, B. (2021). *Oral storytelling workbook: Discovering your story and sharing it with an audience.* Capital Storytelling.

Litan, R. (2020). *Resolved: Debate can revolutionize education and help save our democracy.* Brookings Institution Press.

Lorde, A (2020). Poetry is not a luxury. In R. Gay (Ed.), *The selected works of Audre Lorde* (pp. 3–7). W. W. Norton.

Love, B. L. (2019). *We want to do more than survive: Abolitionist teaching and the pursuit of educational freedom.* Beacon Press.

McDermott, R., Goldman, S., & Varenne, H. (2006). The cultural work of learning disabilities. *Educational Researcher, 35*(6), 12–17.

Najavits, L. M. (2019). *Finding your best self: Recovery from trauma, addiction, or both* (Rev. ed.). Guilford.

National Academies of Sciences, Engineering, and Medicine. (2018). *How people learn II: Learners, contexts, and cultures.* National Academies Press.

National Governors Association Center for Best Practices & Council of Chief State School Officers. (2010). *Common Core State Standards for English language arts & literacy in history/social studies, science, and technical subjects.* http://www.corestandards.org/ELA-Literacy/

Neimand, A., Asorey, N., Christiano, A., & Wallace, Z. (2021, September 29). Why intersectional stories are key to helping the communities we serve. *Stanford Social Innovation Review.* https://ssir.org/articles/entry/why_intersectional_stories_are_key_to_helping_the_communities_we_serve

Nichols, R. G., & Stevens, L. A. (2019). Listening to people. *Harvard Business Review, 27.* https://hbr.org/1957/09/listening-to-people.

Okun, T. (2021). *White supremacy culture characteristics.* https://www.whitesupremacyculture.info/characteristics.html

Peterson, A. (2020, April 6). *Literacy is more than just reading and writing* [blog post]. National Council of Teachers of English (NCTE). https://ncte.org/blog/2020/03/literacy-just-reading-writing/

Rose, C. (1993, May 7). Toni Morrison interview with Charlie Rose.

Rudkin, J. K. (2003). *Community psychology: Guiding principles and orienting concepts.* Prentice Hall.

Schwartz, D. L., & Bransford, J. D. (1998). A time for telling. *Cognition and Instruction, 16*(4), 475–522.

Stanford Center for Professional Development. (2019). How to cultivate a classroom culture that supports constructive conversation. https://learn.stanford.edu/OA-CCC-Content-Article-2019-02-16_LP-Article.html

Steele, D. M., & Cohn-Vargas, B. (2013). *Identity safe classrooms: Places to belong and learn.* Corwin.

Treasure, J. (2011). *5 ways to listen better* [Video]. TED Conferences. https://www.ted.com/talks/julian_treasure_5_ways_to_listen_better

Vygotsky, L. (1978). *Mind in society.* Harvard University Press.

Walkington, L. (2020). Speak about it, be about it: Spoken-word poetry communities and transformative social justice. *Critical Criminology, 29*(3), 649–666.

Index

About the Authors

AnnMarie Baines, PhD, is the founder and executive director of the Bay Area nonprofit organization The Practice Space, which elevates underrepresented voices and supports young people and adults in developing authentic, clear, and engaging voices through public speaking. In addition to more than 20 years of experience coaching public speaking in West Contra Costa, California, and Boston Public Schools, she has held faculty positions at San Francisco State University and UC Berkeley. She is a two-time winner of the competitive Title Nine Pitchfest Nonprofit Edition, and a *Los Angeles Times* Inspirational Woman nominee. Growing up in West Contra Costa as the daughter of a Filipino immigrant, AnnMarie became deeply dedicated to her community and committed to equity as a Deeper Learning Equity Fellow. She was a program officer at the George Lucas Educational Foundation, where she applied her expertise in curriculum, project-based learning, and professional development. AnnMarie received her PhD in learning sciences from University of Washington, her teaching credential from Boston Teacher Residency, and a master's degree in education policy from the Harvard Graduate School of Education.

 **Diana Medina,** a senior staff member at The Practice Space, is a first-generation Mexican American poet, educator, and storyteller born and raised in Los Angeles, California. She has worked in the nonprofit sector uplifting communities of color for the last 16 years. Her mission in life is to use her gift with words to bring more clarity, compassion, and connection to communities in need of healing. Diana holds a bachelor's degree in political science from California State University Northridge and a master's degree in public administration from the University of Southern California. She is an alumna of the Coro Fellowship in Public Affairs and the Education Pioneers Graduate Fellowship. In 2021, Diana released her debut poetry collection *Healing Out Loud* through Alegria Publishing. Her writing has also been featured in *Modern Latina* magazine and StoryCenter. Diana believes all people speak in poems and stories. It is her calling to hear them, write them, speak them, and share them with the world.

 **Caitlin Healy,** a senior staff member at The Practice Space, is an educator with more than 15 years of experience teaching youth of all ages, as well as adults. Before joining The Practice Space team, Caitlin taught social studies for seven years in public schools, where she helped coach teachers on project-based and blended learning. As a program coordinator for San Francisco Peer Resources, she supported high school students by facilitating peer education workshops for more than 1,000 middle and high school students. She has a master's degree in education and a teaching credential from Mills College in Oakland and a bachelor's degree in American studies from UC Santa Cruz. Caitlin uses her background in alternative education to advocate for youth pushed to the margins by public school systems.

Related ASCD Resources

At the time of publication, the following resources were available (ASCD stock numbers in parentheses).

Cultivating Joyful Learning Spaces for Black Girls: Insights into Interrupting School Pushout by Monique W. Morris (#121004)

Demystifying Discussion: How to Teach and Assess Academic Conversation Skills, K–5 by Jennifer Orr (#122003)

Fostering Student Voice (Quick Reference Guide) by Russell Quaglia and Kristine Fox (#QRG119034)

Keeping It Real and Relevant: Building Authentic Relationships in Your Diverse Classroom by Ignacio Lopez (#117049)

Literacy Is Liberation: Working Toward Justice Through Culturally Relevant Teaching by Kimberly N. Parker (#122024)

The Power of Voice in Schools: Listening, Learning, and Leading Together by Russ Qualia, Kristine Fox, Lisa Lande, and Deborah Young (#120021)

Questioning for Classroom Discussion: Purposeful Speaking, Engaged Listening, Deep Thinking by Jackie Acree Walsh and Beth Dankert Sattes (#115012)

Students Taking Action Together: 5 Teaching Techniques to Cultivate SEL, Civic Engagement, and a Healthy Democracy by Lauren M. Fullmer, Laura F. Bond, Crystal N. Molyneaux, Samuel J. Nayman, and Maurice J. Elias (#122029)

Teaching to Empower: Taking Action to Foster Student Agency, Self-Confidence, and Collaboration by Debbie Zacarian and Michael Silverstone (#120006)

Tell Your Story: Teaching Students to Become World-Changing Thinkers and Writers by Ernest Morrell and Pam Allyn (#122031)

Your Students, My Students, Our Students: Rethinking Equitable and Inclusive Classrooms by Lee Ann Jung, Nancy Frey, Douglas Fisher, and Julie Kroener (#119019)

For up-to-date information about ASCD resources, go to www.ascd.org. You can search the complete archives of *Educational Leadership* at www.ascd.org/el. To contact us, send an email to member@ascd.org or call 1-800-933-2723 or 703-578-9600.